"Phil knows what it takes to win. And that is exactly what *Measuring Customer Experience* provides to managers who want their companies to win through building strong relationships with customers."

– Timothy Keiningham, PhD, Global Chief Strategy Officer and
Executive Vice President, Ipsos Loyalty; Bestselling Author of
The Wallet Allocation Rule and Why Loyalty Matters

"Dr. Phil Klaus's investigation and findings on how to measure and improve Customer Experience addresses one of the most pressing issues for marketeers and businesses today. His erudite approach to the subject breaks new ground with the EXQ technique being one that will in due course filter down into the practice of advanced marketeers."

– Crispin Rogers, Director Targeted Marketing, Visa Europe

"Move past individual customer service with this systematic "next-practice" guide to thinking beyond the simple transaction, enhancing your total customer experience and increasing profitability."

– Ian Di Tullio, Director Loyalty Marketing, Air Canada

"Dr. Phil delivers a revolutionary new way to understand and measure the Customer Experience. He was able to challenge the commonly used surveys to propose a method that allows true insight on how to enhance the customer experience, and ultimately increase Customer Lifetime Value."

– Denis Kraus, CDO, Executive Committee, Groupe Beaumanoir

"This well-researched and rigorous book begins with the basics of what customer experience really is and then lays out a systematic process for designing and implementing the most appropriate CX strategies....a valuable resource for both scholars and practitioners."

– Prof. A. "Parsu" Parasuraman, Professor of Marketing &
The James W. McLamore Chair, University of Miami, Marketing Legend

"Dr. Klaus has produced a definitive study of Customer Experience in today's economy that establishes a direct link between CX, sales growth and profitability. The categorization of companies into Vanguards, Transformers and Preservers classifies different organizational approaches and evaluates the behaviors, which lead to higher or lower levels of sales growth over time. By combining academic rigor with practical insight, Dr. Klaus has produced a framework that all companies can implement to measure and design their CX experience across the organization. Dr. Klaus' passion for all aspects of CX translates into a readable study full of genuinely helpful advice for business leaders. The definitive linkage of great CX to improved profitability will help many business leaders win the argument for investment and change within their own companies."

– Chris Combemale, Executive Director,
Direct Marketing Organization (DMA) UK

"This book provides a useful roadmap, addressing the pressing questions managers face: Where are we currently in terms of managing and measuring customer experience? Where do we want to be? And most important, how do we get there?"

– Katherine N. Lemon, PhD, Accenture Professor of Marketing, Chair,
Marketing Department, Carroll School of Management, Boston College

"Professor Klaus delivers a forceful call for business to manage the entire, holistic customer experience (CX), much more than just service quality and customer satisfaction. His message, itself, is holistically crafted, weaving together scholarship and practice; strategy, implementation, and measurement; with links forged to CX quality and profitability."

– David Bowen, Ph.D., Robert and Katherine Herberger Chair in
Global Management and Professor of Management, Thunderbird School
of Global Management Organizational Behavior/HR Thought Leader

"We know that customer loyalty is one of the most important drivers for the business performance, particularly at a professional service firm. However, we didn't know what exactly affected it. Through dedicated research, Phil clearly demonstrated the solution by presenting the conceptual model and measurement tool. This is an excellent book and I strongly recommend this to all the executives involved in measuring everything related to customers."

– Dr. Junichi Kato, Managing Director TMF Group Japan

"*Measuring Customer Experience* offers a simple but insightful guide for managers about on how to deliver performance through effective customer experience management."

– Professor Rod Brodie, University of Auckland,
Marketing Hall of Fame Inductee

"Phil Klaus has written an exciting book well-grounded in theory and in empirical research. Customer experience is an important phenomenon that exponentially gains interest among practitioners and academics alike. The book is provides valuable ideas, structures, and tools. Reading it is a great experience."

– Christian Grönroos, Professor of Service and Relationship Marketing,
Hanken School of Economics, Finland

How to Develop and Execute the Most Profitable Customer Experience Strategies

Measuring Customer Experience

Philipp Klaus

First published 2015 by
PALGRAVE MACMILLAN

Palgrave Macmillan in the UK is an imprint of Macmillan Publishers Limited, registered in England, company number 785998, of Houndmills, Basingstoke, Hampshire RG21 6XS.

Palgrave Macmillan in the US is a division of St Martin's Press LLC, 175 Fifth Avenue, New York, NY 10010.

Palgrave Macmillan is the global academic imprint of the above companies and has companies and representatives throughout the world.

Palgrave® and Macmillan® are registered trademarks in the United States, the United Kingdom, Europe and other countries.

ISBN 978–1–137–37545–2

This book is printed on paper suitable for recycling and made from fully managed and sustained forest sources. Logging, pulping and manufacturing processes are expected to conform to the environmental regulations of the country of origin.

A catalogue record for this book is available from the British Library.

Library of Congress Cataloging-in-Publication Data
Klaus, Philipp.
Measuring customer experience : how to develop and execute the most profitable customer experience strategies / Philipp Klaus.
pages cm
ISBN 978–1–137–37545–2
1. Customer services.   2. Customer satisfaction.   I. Title.
HF5415.5.K5355 2015
658.8'12—dc23   2014029412

Typeset by MPS Limited, Chennai, India.

Contents

10   The Science behind the Knowledge ⁄ 119

List of Figures and Tables

Foreword

Companies around the world have come to recognize the importance of customer experience measurement and management to the ultimate success of their firms. In fact, a 2014 survey of 1020 CEOs from around the world conducted by The Conference Board found that the second most daunting challenge CEOs believed that they faced was building stronger customer relationships. This was second only getting top quality employees capable of performing the work. Perhaps even more shocking, essential success factors like innovation and even operational excellence fell below customer relationships.

To address this need, companies have embraced customer experience management with fervor. An entire industry has developed to support companies on this journey. Professional associations have sprung up for customer experience managers and consultants that can boast thousands of members.

The result of all this is that tens of billions of dollars are spent by companies every year on efforts to measure, analyze, and manage the customer experience. The great news is that this has been an unbridled success, with companies growing rapidly and making record profits; moreover customers are consistently delighted with the companies with which they do business. Sadly, we all know immediately that this statement must be sarcasm as it does not remotely reflect reality.

A major problem is that, despite an understanding of the importance of customer relationships to a company's success and a fervent embrace of customer experience management, managers do not have a good understanding of what customer experience management entails nor do they know precisely what they must do to achieve success.

That is why *Measuring Customer Experience* is so important and timely. Phil Klaus is a renowned customer experience management thought leader. More important, he is one of the very few experts who really understand the science of what works and the management practices required to make it work. Phil is well known in the scientific community for his rigorous research on all things related to company–customer relationships. Before his academic career, however, Phil had a strong career in marketing and management consulting. Perhaps more important to understanding Phil's relentless drive to understand the secrets for success, he is an avid mountain bike racer.

Phil takes the complex and makes it simple. His clear, step-by-step approach will resonate with managers who recognize how complex (and often unwieldy) the process of designing, managing, and measuring customer experience can be. This book provides a useful roadmap, addressing the pressing questions managers face: where are we currently in terms of managing and measuring customer experience? Where do we want to be? And most important, how do we get there? Executives charged with customer experience management—in marketing, operations, information systems, talent management, or the C-suite—will gain valuable insights and practical techniques for improving their customer experience, and linking such improvements to the bottom line.

Whether your organization is just starting its own customer experience journey, or if it is well on its way to delivering excellent, consistent customer experiences, this book is certainly for you. For those just building a customer experience management capability, Phil provides a structure for understanding the dimensions of customer experience that clearly answers the question, "Where do I even start?" For those who have a well-developed customer experience capability in hand, Phil's customer experience management balance sheet and detailed approach to measurement will enable you to accelerate the ROI on your current efforts.

Phil knows what it takes to win. And that is exactly what *Measuring Customer Experience* provides to managers who want their companies to win through building strong relationships with customers.

Timothy Keiningham, PhD
Global Chief Strategy Officer and Executive Vice President, Ipsos Loyalty
Bestselling Author of *The Wallet Allocation Rule* and *Why Loyalty Matters*
Katherine N. Lemon, PhD
Accenture Professor of Marketing, Chair, Marketing Department
Carroll School of Management, Boston College

Preface

Customer experience (hereafter CX) is omnipresent. A quick Google search will deliver 539,000,000 hits. Today there are more than 1,200,000 professionals associated with the term. CX blogs, consultants, programs, workshops, conferences, indexes, frameworks, awards, summits, metrics, Net Promoter Score, mapping, Customer Experience Management – CX is everywhere and widely considered the *next competitive battleground*. Managers, consultants, scholars, and even politicians seem to agree that the age of the customer has finally arrived and we had better be ready for it. The new customer needs new solutions, and blue chip companies like Siemens, IBM, Adobe, and Google are standing by, ready to deliver. Customer Relationship Management is proclaimed dead, and CX management in an area where the customer calls the shots is the declared new silver bullet for companies worldwide. We read the great CX stories of Apple, Amazon, and Starbucks, and are left wondering how this will apply to our business? Moreover, while we still struggle to coherently define what constitutes CX, we already discuss the next generation of CX management, the role of social media, cloud networks in delivering excellent experiences, and follow the CX revolution on YouTube.

It's time to take a deep breath. Yes, CX management is crucial, and we are entering an era where customers call the shots and success will be based on how well companies can rise to meet their demands and expectations. Customers have many choices today. Therefore, it is critical to make their experiences as simple, consistent, and relevant as possible. By delivering the desired customer experiences, companies can acquire new customers, retain more customers, and improve efficiency. However, how can companies accomplish this? First, by clearly defining CX. What is it exactly? What influence does it have on a firm's performance? How can it be measured? How can it be managed? And, if it can be managed, which strategies are the most profitable ones? My book will deliver the answers to these crucial questions.

Compared to others, my book offers a unique, relevant, and rigorous approach. It is based upon the fact that as scholars we only have one master – the truth. Using this approach and multiple global, longitudinal studies *Measuring Customer Experience* delivers unbiased empirical evidence driven by business needs. The book focuses on how you as the key decision-maker can use this knowledge to

a. find evidence why CX management is crucial to your business;
b. learn about the existing CX management strategies and management models and their performance in order to
   - benchmark your business in terms of the five dimensions of CX management practices, and
   - develop and implement a CX strategy delivering superior performance to your business, independent from your company's size, sector, focus, or industry.

Measuring Customer Experience focuses on the process rather than outcomes or storytelling. It delivers easy-to-follow, step-by-step instructions on how you can not only master the challenges of the market, such as changing customer expectations and competitive threats, but also deliver superior performance through CX management.

Measuring Customer Experience will allow you to unlock the Black Box of CX and use this knowledge for the success of your business.

For those of you who would like to jump 'right into action, or are in short supply of time, I suggest the following.

1. If you only have 5 minutes, jump directly to page 75, and take advantage of our exclusive evaluation offer on page 80.
2. CX isn't everything, and can be both measured, and managed. If you want to measure it, scroll right to page 100.
3. Problems with getting a buy-in from the board? Try the 'Trojan Horse' (p. 108) approach.

Still struggling? Read Chapter 9.

Acknowledgments

Acknowledgments are more than just an opportunity to say "thank you." They allow you, the reader, a glimpse of who was working "behind the scenes" to make this book possible. Before I introduce all the people who were essential in seeing an idea of mine through to fruition, I, and every single one of us, want to thank you for considering our work worth reading. We are much obliged.

Allow me to thank former Editor Eleanor Davey Corrigan, who contacted me initially to discuss the project and get the ball rolling, so to say. I am grateful for the support of the team at Palgrave Macmillan, in particular Publisher Tamsine O'Riordan, and Josie Taylor, who always shared a word of support, and demonstrated flexibility whenever I needed it most. I am indebted to the marketing and PR team and their relentless efforts in promoting the book, and coming up with such a great cover.

I want to acknowledge the crucial support of my peers. Even if there is only one name on the book's cover, the research driving the insights I am sharing is based upon the relentless efforts and support from my colleagues. While there are too many to mention, I want to give a special cheer to Stan Maklan. I am indebted to him for our countless discussions, which were a driving force in developing my research agenda. Thanks are also due to Bo Edvardsson, my kind and always encouraging mentor. Without your guidance, ongoing support, and friendship, I wouldn't be where I am today. Permit me to say thank you to my colleagues who have been instrumental in both my personal development, and the development of the CX Research agenda: Malcolm Kirkup, Tim Keiningham, Paul Baines, Kay Lemon, Thorsten Gruber, and Anders Gustaffson.

Last, but by no means least, I give my heartfelt thanks to the ones without whom this book would never have seen the light of day. The ones who gave a comforting smile and a "C'mon, Daddy," when all the extra work seemed to overwhelm me. This book is dedicated to my beloved wife, Claudia, and our two children – our son, Elliot, and our daughter, Vivi. Without you and your selfless time and care, which were sometimes the only things that kept me going, no one would be able to read these lines. I love you more than I can ever express in words. You are what drives me, nourishes me, and you are the light of my life. In addition, please forgive me for not spending enough time with you during the writing of this book, or as Elliot would say, "No work, Daddy, let's play together." Let's play!

Ti voglio bene

The author wants to thank the CTF Service Research Center at Karlstad University, Cranfield University School of Management, and Polytechnic University of Bari (Prof. Gorgolione) for their generous financial support for some of the research included in this book.

chapter 1

Customer Experience: The Origins and Importance for Your Business

Today's organizations have a new, overarching, and often overwhelming challenge to successfully manage the customer experience. This challenge ranges from seeking how to create compelling customer experiences through all stages of the customer's engagement, to managing the customer's expectations and assessing it, before, during, and after the buying process (Berry et al. 2002). There is widespread agreement that customer experience is different from, and more complex than, service quality (e.g., Schembri 2006) and customer satisfaction (e.g., Verhoef et al. 2009), and that it is context specific (Lemke et al. 2011). This makes it difficult for scholars, researchers, and consultants both to assist managers in understanding customer experience and suggest generic "best practice" to them. It is therefore up to managers to interpret this emerging concept and make sense of its implementation (Maklan & Klaus 2011).

In order to understand Customer Experience (CX), we need to first explore its origins – the history of the phenomenon. Understanding the history of the CX concept is important as it will allow us not only to see how

CX evolved over time, but also give us the ability to learn from others' choices, mistakes, and opportunities. CX management is about applying knowledge, and managers are wise if they use knowledge that someone created and applied before them. After all, an intelligent man learns from his own mistakes, but a wise man learns from others' mistakes. Learning about how researchers viewed, explored, and defined CX in the past is important so we can start where they left off and move on, instead of just repeating what they did.

To survive in today's economy, offering high-quality goods and services alone is not sufficient. Companies have to compete on a more complex level by creating a satisfactory customer experience through all stages of the buying process, managing the customer's expectations and assessments before, during, and after the sale.

Definitions of CX are truly broad. They range from a customer's actual and anticipated purchase and consumption experience, a distinctive economic offering or the result of encountering, undergoing, or living through things, to the notion of the new, experience-seeking consumer as co-creator of value and experience. The term "co-creation" highlights the influence of customer experience on experiential marketing strategies, such as the ones desired and executed in the luxury goods/services, tourism, travel, and hospitality contexts.

Research links customer experience to most of the outcomes that managers want to measure, or, are actively measuring. These may be intentions and a customer's state-of-mind (e.g., customer satisfaction, a customer's intention to become and/or stay loyal, or the likelihood of them giving a recommendation), or actual behavior (e.g., actively recommending the firm's offerings, purchasing, and repurchasing behavior, share-of-category, or word-of-mouth behavior). However, while the phenomenon of customer and consumption experience can be traced back as far as to the contributions of economists Adam Smith and Alfred Marshall in the early twentieth century, the recent significant number of managerial, academic, and consultancy publications in the field still lacks both a solid foundation and coherent messages about the nature, and more importantly, the management of customer experience. By this I refer to the fact that we still cannot grasp CX's true meaning – what CX actually is, and how to explore knowledge leading to managerial actions.

Psychologists, consumer behavioralists, business, management, and marketing scholars, philosophers, economists, managers, and consultants try to approach and make sense of customer experience from their unique viewpoints. *Measuring Customer Experience* provides you with an extensive review of what has been written about CX as of today. The following historical summary and evolving categories reveal and explain the different CX perspectives and their crucial interconnections.

Table 1.1 shows the structure of the literature review, indicating a broad chronological representation of the CX literature. However, the categorization into ten streams does not imply a smooth evolution from one stream of research to another. These streams are not mutually exclusive – some are complementary and overlap. These ten streams of literature are subsequently divided into three categories, *content*, *process*, and *practice*, which represent the main foci – a typology – of CX thinking (see Table 1.1).

The *content category* is concerned with describing different concepts of CX, establishing its foundations and representing different theoretical views

TABLE 1.1 Customer experience research foci

Category	Literature streams
Content – The concept of customer experience	Economic perspectives
	"Rational" cognitive theories
	Experiential "emotional" theorists and the role of affect
	Peak experiences
Process – How customer experiences arise and evolve	Unidirectional perspectives of customer experience
	Co-created experiences
	Dialogical perspectives
	Brand communities and customer experience
Practice – The portrayal of customer experience management literature	Consultant/analyst perspectives of customer experience
	Services marketing perspectives

about it. The *process category* includes a range of perspectives on how the customer experience arises and evolves during interactions with consumers. The *process category* builds on the research discussed in the content section, emphasizing the role and degree of involvement of the customer experience provider and the customer in designing and influencing the customer experience. The *practice category* assesses the CX practice and CX management literature. This category includes the newer contributions of recent service marketing and CX research, positioning customer experience as a new competitive imperative for companies, leading to insights on how to successfully measure and therefore manage it.

Content – the concept of CX

Economic perspectives – first traces

The importance of customer experience as the driver of consumption has been indicated in the early economic literature (e.g., Keynes 1936), in which it is described as the measure on which consumers decide what goods and resulting experiences to purchase (Parsons 1934).

The power of rationality

Despite these early acknowledgments of the importance of customer experience as a "sufficient choice criterion" (Howard & Sheth 1969, p. 26) for buyers' behavior, the rational (i.e., cognitive-focused) examinations of early behavioral researchers insisted on explaining consumer actions as a purely rational cognitive process (e.g., Ajzen & Fishbein 1977). This view, linking cognition, affect, and behavior (CAB), suggests that customers are involved in a rational assessment of their past, present, and imagined future experience and use this information to determine their behavioral intentions. According to CAB, customers base their decision process on a sequential rational assessment of expectations versus outcomes (e.g., Gronroos 1997). CAB researchers believe that customers collect sufficient information to evaluate choices by constantly assessing their expectations one by one, which, in turn, drives their intentions. However, despite complications and inconsistencies in their conceptualization, CAB researchers uphold their definition of rational consumer behavior as the leading theory in buying behavior. Predictably, experiential researchers challenged this notion.

It's not all brain – the role of emotions

Experiential researchers suggest that emotions play a, if not *the*, critical role in consumer behavior. Subsequently, they re-introduce the significance of emotions, and the emotional customer experiences in consumer behavior (e.g., Hirschman & Holbrook 1982). This shift towards a non-utilitarian focus to explain consumer choices is supported by the distinction between buying and consuming behavior, affirming that using a product or service (i.e., the customer experience), will ultimately determine a consumer's choice (Alderson 1957). This transference from the functions towards the hedonistic properties of products and services highlights emotions' importance for CX management (Klaus 2011).

The fascination of the extraordinary

Building upon emotional factors as a cornerstone to explain consumer behavior, researchers now turned their focus towards the differences in these emotional experiences. From this research two streams of knowledge emerged: extraordinary experiences and the overall assessment of customer experience (Klaus & Maklan 2011). Extraordinary experiences research, based on a social science framework, challenges the notion of the traditional, service-quality-grounded thinking that the customer experience is a summation of all the elements of a *holistic* customer experience (Verhoef et al. 2009). Extraordinary experiences research refers to the idea that, while encountering extraordinary experiences, such as the often-cited river rafting experience (Arnould & Price 1993), tourism, vacations, dining, being in entertainment parks, and taking part in sports and leisure activities, consumers both cannot and do not follow the traditional confirmation–disconfirmation paradigm facing these experiences (Klaus & Maklan 2011). This paradigm states that customers simply judge their experiences by comparing their expectations to their perceptions. Among extraordinary experiences, the most developed categories are flow and peak experiences. Schouten et al. (2007) coined the term "transcendent customer experience" to refer to flow and/or peak experiences. Flow experiences occurrences are events in which we are completely involved in an activity for its own sake. Our ego takes a backseat, time flies, every action inevitably follows the previous one, and we are completely involved. This is often referred to as "being in a zone," and can occur during creative activities (e.g., drawing or writing) or while engaging in the sport of our choice. Peak experiences are often described as moments of pure joy and excitement – moments that stand out from everyday events. People often connect the lasting memories of peak experiences with a spiritual, even divine, experience. Both flow, and peak experiences are related (Privette 1983) and sometimes overlap in the same activities. Carù and Cova (2003) highlight, though, that we should not forget about the ordinary experiences and their interlink relationship with extraordinary experiences. Their key message is that without comparing ordinary experiences derived from our daily mundane life – in fact, benchmarking them – no experience can be called "extraordinary." Thus, those ordinary experiences are also important parts of our lives, and can consist of different levels of intensity. As a result, researchers propose that the customer experience exists on an ever-shifting continuum between ordinary to extraordinary, rather than being mutually exclusive to either one (Klaus and Maklan 2011).

While we can establish that customers' actions are more and more experience-driven, this fact provides little guidance to managers to determine which kind of experience drives which kind of behavior at which particular stage. Managers often do not know if and when the design of extraordinary experiences is required to drive the important behavior they are looking for, such as purchasing, repurchasing, loyalty, and positive word-of-mouth. Moreover, if experiences are indeed a blend between extraordinary and ordinary experiences, how can managers understand at which stage and through which channel, these different experiences need to be designed and delivered? Perhaps the knowledge of how experiences arise and evolve – the customer experience process – can provide us with some answers to these burning questions?

Process – how customer experiences arise and evolve

Based upon the findings of the kinds of customer experiences consumers can have, researchers moved on to explore the various perspectives on how the customer experience arises and evolves during the interactions between the firm, their channels, their products, their employees, their products and services, and consumers (e.g., Schmitt 2003). In particular, the role and degree of involvement of the CX provider and the customer in designing, delivering, and influencing the customer experience have stimulated multiple research domains.

Let's get together – from unidirectional to co-creation

The research ranges from a more provider-driven, unidirectional (the firm's) perspective to customer-driven, co-created experiences (Palmer 2010). On the one hand, researchers suggest that every firm can, with the support of their customers, aim to carefully craft the delivery of a customer experience (Payne et al. 2008). This perspective highlights the role of knowledge-sharing processes, as the firm seeks to understand every facet of the customer experience throughout all direct and indirect encounters and interaction with their existing and potential customers (Frow & Payne 2007). And, let's be quite clear, both viewpoints (the firm's and their customers') play a vital role in developing, executing, measuring, and managing the customer experience. On the other hand, researchers indicate that the involvement of customers in the experience design and management process will add little more than costs, and con-firmation of already existing knowledge. Or as the Chief Marketing Officer (CMO) of a telecommunication company mentioned in an interview with me, "We already know what they [the customers] want. They want it cheaper, faster, and more reliable. How could that possibly help us?" Other internal market research groups, such as consumer electronics, raise similar questions by highlighting that often consumer simply "don't know what they really want. So, how could this help us in our research and development process?" In addition, of course, there is always the notion of managers just knowing their customers "better than they do themselves."

However, a famous study highlights that while 80 percent of Chief Executive Officers (CEOs) claim they deliver great customer experiences, only 8 percent of their customers agreed with this judgment.

Co-creating experiences requires interactions between the customer and the firm. While researchers link these approaches with customer experience, sometimes the connection is vague (Klaus & Maklan 2011). Unlike the peak experience perspective, the co-creation perspective regards the customer experience holistically, including all interactions in a sequential order (Payne et al. 2008). Co-creation considers every interaction as imperative to the customers' evaluation of their experience (Ballantyne & Varey 2006). The function of the firm is therefore to facilitate the customers' ability to attain an optimal experience (LaSalle & Britton 2003). One limitation of the co-creation idea is its insufficient explanation of the impact of social context on the customer experience, such as peer-to-peer interactions. We all know how influential these peer-to-peer, or, if you like, consumer-to-consumer/customer-to-customer interactions are. Just think about the power of peer review in e-commerce, or the influence of rating websites such as TripAdvisor. An individual experience of a product or service may be highly dependent on the social experience of a group or wider social context (Gentile et al. 2007). After all, we experience having dinner by ourselves, with our loved ones, or with a group of friends, in entirely different ways, simply because of the company (or lack of it) we are in. Researchers argue that the social context, perhaps more accurately labeled as the "customer context," indicates that the customer experience is dependent on customer, other customers, and service provider alike (e.g., Mascarenhas et al. 2006). Brand community research is another domain providing some useful insights into the customer context aspect of the customer experience (Schouten et al. 2007) by highlighting the community aspect, which we today find so often in social media. However, the research often fails to identify how membership in a brand community changes the overall customer experience, and, more importantly, consumer behavior. Christensen et al. (2005) expand on this literature by submitting that the context – defined as what customers are trying to accomplish, independent from the service provider – can affect the customer experience. Imagine you simply want to get a job done: For example, after researching which tablet you want to buy, you simply want to walk into the airport store and purchase it for the advertised price. No hassle, no sales talk, no additional insurance, no set-up required, no other requests. You simply want to buy the tablet and get on the plane. However, the service person follows their script and asks you all these questions: "Are you certain you want this one?" "Have you seen this one?" "Can I offer you this one?" and so on. In this case, your experience might not be a good one. Now imagine scenario two: You walk into the same store, but you aren't certain yet which tablet you want to buy. The same service person and approach might now be offering exactly the guidance and information you are looking for. You most likely will have a good experience, and leave the shop with a tablet, too. In both cases, you were looking to purchase the same tablet, and you did, but your experiences, and the likelihood of sharing them, and the likelihood of returning to the store are on the opposite sides of the spectrum. And this depended solely on the experience you were looking for, not the product, not the price, not the service personnel, and not the store location.

Another approach in exploring the influence of customer experience is to discover the roles of multiple stakeholders (Roper & Davies 2007). This perspective draws attention to the fact that the customer and firm relationship is only one of many relationships important in creating the customer experience (Verhoef et al. 2009). It suggests that understanding the customer experience involves identifying the influence of all stakeholders in creating the customer experience. The contribution of this research is the added, socially constructed focus, and therefore enriched understanding, of the customer experience. However, we still need to determine which offerings need to incorporate the influences of these stakeholder interactions in their CX design. While process research delivers some interesting insights into if – and if yes, how – the firm, the customers, and other stakeholders can interact and eventually create experiences together, it also raises many questions. For example: When is a more unidirectional, transactional management practice more appropriate than an experience-based one? How can a firm determine and influence the importance of peer-to-peer interactions? Will other stakeholders be a part of the customer experience design? If yes, which ones, and in what capacity? In the following we now take a look at how today's firms practice CX and what we can learn from them.

Practice – portrayal of CX management literature

CX is not explicitly discussed in the context of marketing practices, and rightfully so, because it is, after all, a strategic initiative. However, there is an emerging practices literature within the marketing discipline, which follows work in other disciplines such as sociology, anthropology (Garfinkel 1967), and social philosophy (Schatzki 1996). Most of the marketing literature, is focused on either the "entertainment" aspects of the customer experience (Pine & Gilmore 1999) or on managerial outcomes and actions (e.g., Berry et al. 2002).

The impact of customer experience on business has not been discussed in the marketing literature until recently (Prahalad & Ramaswamy 2004). Creating superior customer experiences is seen as one of the key objectives for the success of the organization (Verhoef et al. 2009). Organizations are elevating the management of customer experiences to a top-priority item in their efforts to build customer loyalty in brands, channels, and services (Badgett et al. 2007). Managing customer experience quality has become a crucial strategic ingredient for all organizations. In contrast to the recognition of the importance of the CX concept for organizations, the focus of traditional marketing literature has been the measurement of customer satisfaction and service quality (Verhoef et al. 2009). However, some scholars are now challenging the current definition of service quality, its usefulness, and its corresponding measures (Schembri 2006). They believe that customer experience is the key determinant of service quality evaluation. Berry et al. state that "by definition, a good customer experience is good customer service, thus the customer experience is the service" (2006, p. 1).

More than just service ...

Whilst scholars, researchers, and managers acknowledge that experience should be the new focus of managerial attention, they are less unified on both its precise definition and its measure. This creates a dilemma for developing strategies and managing the customer experience (Klaus & Maklan 2007; Klaus 2011). Whilst acknowledging that firms are competing, increasingly, on the basis of customer experience, it is defined imprecisely and, as yet, there are no widely agreed measures of the concept (Maklan & Klaus 2011). More recent research indicates that customers evaluate the value of a product or service through the process of usage rather than at the moment of exchange (e.g., Tynan et al. 2010). Therefore, the product or service quality assessed at the point of purchase is necessary but not sufficient to determine the value of the product or service (Vargo & Lusch 2004). True value (Woodruff 1997), according to the marketing literature, is to be obtained through use (Woodruff & Flint 2006). For services, especially, value is often produced after the service encounter, as in the use of knowledge acquired on an executive course, applied at a later stage (Edvardsson et al. 2005), or a patient following advice by a medical clinician (McColl-Kennedy et al. 2009). Even in contexts such as entertainment, where the hedonic experience constitutes the service delivery (Murray & Bellmann 2011), the experience can be influenced by contextual factors such as the presence of other customers, and subsequently cannot be viewed as having been created exclusively by the service company (e.g., Schembri 2009). One stream of research identifies experiential factors to be a key component of customer experience, but these are missing from the construct of service quality (Lee & Lin 2005).

An alternative research stream distinguishes between service quality and customer experience by challenging the definition of service quality and its commercial application, the Rater questionnaire and measurements as an overall appraisal (Zeithaml 1988). Voss, Roth, and Chase (2008) point out that service quality focuses on a transaction-specific appraisal rather than the concept of the customer journey, described as the customer's sequence of touch-points with the company in buying and obtaining service – a prevalent notion in service design (Berry et al. 2002, Voss et al.

2008). This notion, while verifying the definition of service quality in that a customer's perception may fluctuate during the journey (Schembri 2006), refines its static measurement. Cowley (2008), for example, shows that service encounters may be assessed retrospectively as more positive in order to rationalize a desired purchase. Payne et al. (2008) promote the idea that service experience goes further than the construct of service quality by observing that the customer journey may both precede the service encounter and continue after it. Other scholars draw on this work and propose an even further differentiation between service quality and the customer's service experience. For example, Payne et al. (2008) raise awareness of the fact that the customer experience includes not only communication and usage, but also service encounters. As a result, if it is suggested that customers evaluate their experience holistically (Verhoef et al. 2009). Analogous holistic frameworks have been put forward (Payne et al. 2008; Grewal et al. 2009), leading to calls for empirical assessments of the customer experience (Voss et al. 2008). In one of these consequent studies, Klaus and Maklan (2012) conclude that managing the customer experience is indeed different from managing customer service quality, which focuses upon single service episodes under the control of the company.

While many scholars and practitioners acknowledge that experience should be the new focus of managerial attention, they are less unified on both its precise definition and its scope. This creates a dilemma for developing strategies, managing customer experience, and identifying best practice.

Services marketing perspectives

Service marketing literature concerned with the theoretical construct of customer experience, rather than managerial outcomes, is limited (Verhoef et al. 2009) and based on the notion that customer experience is a summation of all the clues a consumer receives from all direct and indirect interaction with a firm and their offerings, which add somehow to an overall experience (Mossberg 2007). This conceptualization of customer experience has been explored more recently, suggesting the *holistic* and *total* nature of the customer experience (Meyer & Schwager 2007). Meyer and Schwager (2007, p. 118) define customer experience as "the internal and subjective response customers have to any direct or indirect contact with a company."

Gentile et al. (2007) conducted empirical research on the role of experiential features of well-known brands and their products, such as Ikea and Nike. Their research suggests that the different components for understanding the customer experience include sensorial, emotional, cognitive, pragmatic (practically doing something), lifestyle, and relational components. By investigating the role of different experiential features in the success achieved by some products, their research suggests that a value proposition should include both experiential features (hedonic, experiential value) and functional characteristics (utilitarian/functional value).

This notion is similar to the findings of Schmitt (1999), who suggests that customer experience is based on different components important for engaging the customer at different levels: sense, feel, cognitive, physical experiences, lifestyle, and the customer's social identity relative to a reference group. Still, companies receive little assistance on how to incorporate all these levels in managing the customer experience. Palmer (2010, p. 198) likewise posits that "the challenge for the development of a customer experience construct is to integrate a typically diverse array of stimuli in order to assess the trade-offs that are entailed in creating value for consumers." Stimuli present in a customer experience are typically interactive, and it has been pointed out by Csikszentmihalyi (1988) that the manner in which these stimuli are combined and sequenced is important in defining consumer experience, further complicating the matter of CX management.

Verhoef et al. (2009) suggest that the customer experience is of a cognitive, social, affective, and physical nature. Their model of customer experience creation suggests that the determinants of the customer experience, and the corresponding management strategy, include social environment, service interface, retail atmosphere, assortment; price, customer experiences in alternative channels, and the retail brand. Verhoef et al. (2009) state that the situation of the customer experience (e.g., type of store, location) and the consumer themself (e.g., attitudes, task-orientation) can moderate the overall customer experience. This model also reflects the work of other researchers, proposing the nature of customer experience as the customer's response to all direct and indirect encounters with a company (Gentile et al. 2007; Meyer & Schwager 2007).

Verhoef et al.'s (2009) customer experience creation framework, while quite comprehensive, as stated in the holistic description of the customer experience, fails to provide empirical support for their construct. Patricio et al. (2011) argue that experiences may be formed through interactions with multiple services from multiple organizations that go beyond the firm's offerings, and that we cannot only focus on isolated offerings. We need to "contextualize the firm's service concept into the larger context of the value constellation experience and open new forms of service innovation" (p. 197). The implications of this research on the individual company and their CX management, however, are rather broad in nature. Moreover, scholars suggest that customer experience, and therefore CX management, is context-specific (e.g., Lemke et al. 2011). Research exploring which context requires which CX management is, literally, non-existent.

Ask the experts – consultancy research

The CX management practice field has developed very quickly in business practice. In order to contribute to both the scholarly and managerial understanding of CX management practice, it is crucial to include the current state of knowledge from research reports and white papers from business. This research is particularly relevant to the CX management discussion, given its recent and rapidly evolving nature. I focus on the period between 2010 and 2013, comprising reports from leading consultants and researchers: McKinsey, Forrester Research, Boston Consulting Group, Bain & Company, Accenture, Capgemini, KPMG, Ernst & Young, IBM, and the Temkin Group. The majority of the reports are of a conceptual rather than empirical nature, while the latter, unlike scholarly research, often do not discuss the method by which the findings and conclusions were derived in detail, if at all. Both conceptual and empirical studies focus on three main themes: best practice (e.g., Springer et al. 2011), how CX management relates to certain outcomes, and a combination of the two to introduce a tool or framework, such as customer-journey mapping (Rawson et al. 2013). The reports that define customer experience, just like academic research, favor the notion of the customer's perception of all interactions with the firm (e.g., Klaus 2013). The reports can be roughly divided into those written from either the customer's or the firm's viewpoint. The customer's view reports elaborate on how this should shape CX management practices. The consultants often focus on a particular approach to translate this knowledge into action (e.g., Girouard et al. 2012). The firm's view reports often focus on one particular area of possible improvement, such as partner alignment (Hagen 2013). In contrast to academic literature that explores definitions, antecedents, and consequences of CX, the practitioner focus is on tools and best practice that improve performance in one specific (manageable) area/context of CX management. The current practitioner literature therefore lacks a holistic perspective that embraces all facets of CX practice, including its strategic role.

The emerging CX concept, aimed at guiding CX strategy and CX management, is broader than the limited functional service encounter suggested by current measures. It includes pre- and post-service encounter/purchase/consumption experiences, addresses emotional as well as functional dimensions of quality, and includes the customer's social context. It includes an assessment of value-in-use, is formed over multiple channels, and varies with context (Lemke et al. 2011).

However, these holistic concepts of CX are often too broad in nature and are therefore not suitable to support organizations in successfully managing customer experiences and developing CX strategies. Klaus and Maklan's (2012) measurement of customer experience quality (EXQ) captures not only all facets of the construct of the customer experience, but measures the impact of the distinctive drivers of the customer experience on each of the components of the customer experience. They conclude, "Managing the customer experience is, therefore, different from managing customer service which focuses upon single service episodes under the control of the organization" (Klaus & Maklan 2012). This apparent new emphasis of the literature begs the question of whether we are witnessing an emerging shift from service quality towards customer experience. And if this is indeed the case, what does customer experience add to our understanding of what drives loyalty, customer satisfaction, and word-of-mouth?

What does this leave us with ...?

This first chapter has delivered a broad understanding of the origins of CX research and knowledge, and how it evolved over time. The aim is to learn about how researchers viewed, explored, and defined CX in the past so that we can start where they left off and move on, instead of just repeating what they did.

Each of the streams we explored gave us valuable insights, but also left us with important management questions, which still need to be answered in order to achieve what we are after – measuring, and therefore successfully managing, the customer experience.

The more we know, the more we need to know

We know that goods and services are simply a means to an end; they have no value in and of themselves. People buy goods and services to have experiences, not the other way around. But, how effectively and over how long a time frame can consumers assess their end goals and the utilitarian value of an offering?

We are aware that customers' rational information processing alone is not sufficient to guide (and explain) their behavior. So, how do consumers assess and trade off between the emotional and rational aspects of an experience? Moreover, will this assessment vary depending on the context and the offering? And if yes, how and when will this variance occur? Managers need to be able to determine when emotional and when rational factors are more important to both the customer experience and the customer decision.

We learned that extraordinary experiences represent a boundary condition upon the traditional confirmation–disconfirmation paradigm of how consumers assess their experiences. This leads us to the question of how managers delineate between peak and mundane experiences in designing their customer experience practice. Extreme sports are clearly peak experiences, but, more practically, managers need to assess when and how shopping can become more peak than mundane, or vice versa.

We identified that customer experience varies significantly in depth and length from assessments of customer satisfaction and service quality. Customer experience starts before the purchase/consumption of an offering, and lasts way beyond the point of sale and consumption into the time frame of using the product and service. This raises the question of what is a meaningful time frame over which a firm needs to assess customer experience. To what extent does a firm need to manage the experience? Moreover, we explored how other peers/customers have an indirect, but often significant, influence on others' customer experience. However, the question of which and how much of the customer's indirect experiences are relevant to their assessment of the experience is difficult to answer. Even if we can answer this question, how do we manage, and account for, the influence of others on the individual's customer experience?

While we now are aware that a traditional, transaction-based view of how customers obtain value through simple exchange is flawed, we don't know in which context (if any) an exchange-based managerial view (and corresponding strategy) of value is more appropriate than one based on customer experience.

Researchers have established the consumer/customer as the ultimate value assessor and creator; hence, customer experiences are always co-created. However, the extent to which the customer wants to co-create and the capabilities the customer can contribute to the co-creation are not quite so clear.

We live in a brave new world where communication is related to learning and occurs in a many-to-many conversation that is not always mediated or controlled by the focal firm – the power is shifted towards the consumer. This dialogue replaces the dominant persuasion paradigm of marketing communications. Managers are struggling with this power shift, and wonder how they can parse a long-term relationship into manageable dialogues that can be assessed for their impact upon the customer experience. What exact role will the firm play in these dialogues? Is the optimal approach to observe, to mediate, to engage with their customers, or use any possible combination of all these options?

Consultants and market researchers identify customer experience as the next competitive marketing arena and the basis for organizing a firm's activities. Their research provides case-based, best practice examples. However, how managers can construct a business case for an CX investment is not clear. Is more (experience) always better?

So, where does this leave us? The current status quo of customer experience research pushes managers to accept a vast increase in responsibility for customer outcomes at a risk of CX becoming "a theory and practice of everything" (see Table 1.2). Managers don't find this vision either satisfactory or desirable. How can the CX management challenge be approached? This is how, we take the best of all worlds and combine it to gain true insight. We take the academic rigor, managerial insight, and consultants' knowledge, and explore HOW firms today manage the customer experience. Using these insights, we can then classify firms. Understanding the range of CX practices will help managers to evaluate their own practices and determine investment priorities, and provide a clear link to profitability. Profitability is, after all, the firm's ultimate goal. In the next chapter I dissect and cluster existing CX management practices, delivering the foundation for all your CX aims.

TABLE 1.2 Key customer experience research and managerial challenges

1.1 Category	1.2 Literature Streams	1.3 Example Literature	Key Findings or Conclusions *	1.4 Important Management Questions
Content The concept of customer experience	Economic perspectives	Keynes (1936) Parsons (1934)	Goods are a means to an end utility, not valuable in and of themselves.	How effectively and over how long a time frame can consumers assess their end goals/utility?
	Rational cognitive theories of traditional Cognition, Affect, Behavior (CAB)	Fishbein and Ajzen (1976) Sheppard et al. (1988)	Assumes consumers are rational information processors able to assess the consequences of their decisions against the cost when purchasing.	How do customers asses and trade off between emotional and rational aspects of experience, and how does this vary by context?
	Experiential "emotional" theorists and the role of affect	Hirschmann and Holbrook (1982)	Hedonic consumption posits that value is generated from experiences, not the acquisition of goods; people consume experiences using emotional and hedonic faculties.	In which circumstances are hedonic and emotional factors most important to consumers?
	Peak or immersive	Arnould and Price (1993)	Out-of-the-ordinary experiences represent a boundary condition upon the traditional confirmation–disconfirmation theory of how consumers assess experiences.	How do we delineate between peak and mundane experiences in practice? Extreme sports are clearly peak experiences, but, more practically, when and how can shopping become more peak than mundane?

(continued)

TABLE 1.2 Continued

1.1 Category	1.2 Literature Streams	1.3 Example Literature	Key Findings or Conclusions *	1.4 Important Management Questions
	Total, or holistic	Verhoef (2009)	Identifies the depth and length of consumer experience in the context of retail.	What is a meaningful time frame over which a firm needs to assess customer experience? To what extent does a firm need to manage the experience? How much of customers' indirect experiences are relevant to their assessment of the experience?
Process How customer experience arises and evolves	Unidirectional perspectives	Kotler (1991)	Traditional transaction-based view of customers obtaining value through the exchange of goods.	In which contexts (if any) is an exchange-based view of value a more appropriate perspective for managerial decision-making than an experience-based view?
	Co-creation	Vargo and Lusch (2004)	Establishes the customer (consumer) as the ultimate creator of value, hence experiences are co-created.	To what extent does the customer wish to co-create? What capabilities can the customer contribute to co-creation?

(continued)

TABLE 1.2   Continued

1.1 Category	1.2 Literature Streams	1.3 Example Literature	Key Findings or Conclusions *	1.4 Important Management Questions
	Dialogical perspectives	Ballantyne and Varey (2006)	Communication is related to learning and occurs in a many-to-many conversations, which are not always mediated by the focal firm. Such dialogue replaces the dominant persuasion paradigm of marketing communications.	How should managers parse a long-term relationship into manageable dialogues that can be assessed for their impact upon experience? What is the optimal role for the firm to play in dialogues amongst customers?
	Brand communities	McAlexander (2002) Shouten and McAlexander (1995)	Descriptive contributions to the impact of shared experience on consumer experience and brand engagement.	To what extent can firms manage the indirect influences of peers upon the experience?
Practice How customer experience is managed	Consultant/ practitioner	Pine and Gilmore (1999) Schmitt (2003)	Identifies customer experience as the next competitive marketing arena and the basis for organizing a firm's activities.	Practitioner-based articles provide case-based best practice. However, how managers can construct a business case for investment is not clear. Is more (experience) always better?
	Services Marketing Perspectives	Prahalad and Ramaswamy (2004)	Co-creation of experiences is the basis of consumer value. The customer phenomenologically determines value.	How do firms orchestrate complex experience networks?

chapter 2

CX Strategies and Management Practices

We know from the points discussed in Chapter 1 that implementing a CX strategy is challenging. CX's suffers from its broad, holistic definition; it covers an extended time frame, every customer touch point, and both emotional and functional responses. Managers, in order to master this challenge, need to define a clear scope that matches their strategy, and determine an achievable plan to develop it. Given the suggested contextual nature of CX, it is unlikely that researchers will be able to develop a comprehensive and universal guide to CX implementation quickly. Similarly, consultants will not find it easy to develop universal best practices to reduce the risk of failed implementations. The vast majority of scholars exhort managers to do everything they can, based on the unchallenged assumption that only the truly committed and ambitious will succeed (Prahalad & Hamel 1990). However, a large-scale, comprehensive CX program may be beyond the immediate reach of most firms, and may not be considered desirable by all companies on account of their individual strategies. Just think about budget airlines, such as Ryanair, where the customer experience is not considered to be an integral strategic factor. Thus, what is the best approach to master these challenges? First, we need to establish a typology of CX practice based upon how firms actually strategize, practice, and manage their customer experience programs. This typology allows managers to define a level of ambition, scope their efforts, and calibrate their investment accordingly. A typology of CX management is therefore an ideal starting point for firms that want to understand the quality of existing CX practice and plan for CX development systematically.

A typology of CX management is therefore an ideal starting point for firms that want to understand the quality of existing CX practice and plan for CX development systematically

Typologies are a useful approach for thinking about management strategies. Doty and Glick (1994) argue that when "properly developed and fully specified, [typologies] are complex theories that can be subjected to rigorous empirical testing" (p. 231). A CX strategy and management practice typology is therefore a systematic classification of all existing practices in order to understand how these practices work, and, in a subsequent stage, how the different practices relate to profitability.

How we did it … the method

I am aware that the audience for *Measuring Customer Experience* ranges from scholars to managers, but I strongly believe that it is important to demonstrate and share the rigor leading to the typology. My colleagues and I used expert informant interviews to generate data about the meaning of CX management practice and the boundaries of the domain it covers. Our research protocol follows that suggested for exploratory work in well-cited research (e.g., Ericsson & Crutcher 1990). Moreover, the protocol is based on a comprehensive literature review and extant studies exploring marketing practice (Coviello et al. 2002) (see Figure 2.1).

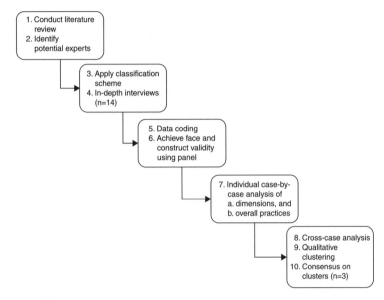

Research protocol

Who we interviewed … the sample

We identified potential experts, following the procedures advocated in the literature (e.g., Hora and Von Winterfeldt 1997), based on the following criteria: (a) tangible evidence of expertise; (b) reputation; (c) availability and willingness to participate; (d) understanding of the general problem area; (e) impartiality; and (f) the lack of an economic or personal stake in the potential findings. Managers in companies representing different industries (see Table 2.1) were selected based upon these criteria: (a) their firm has a recognized customer experience program; (b) they have been employed since its introduction; (c) they have been involved with the program's creation and introduction; and (c) they are responsible for current CX management and program development. This selection procedure ensures a range of views, controls bias (Adelman & Bresnick 1992), and draws on expertise about the phenomenon in question (Ericsson & Crutcher 1990).

TABLE 2.1 Sample profile

Informant	Industry	Country	Title	Years Operating a CX program	Scope
1	Airline	Spain	Vice President Quality Management	>5	National/ B2B/B2C
2	Telecommunications	Spain	Marketing Vice President	>5	Multi-national/ B2B/B2C
3	Automotive	Germany	CMO	>5	Global/ B2C
4	Petrol	U.K.	Head of Retail Business	>5	Global/ B2C
5	Online Banking	Sweden	CMO	>5	Multi-national/ B2C
6	Corporate Banking	Italy	Head of Customer Intelligence	>5	National/ B2B
7	Professional Services	United Kingdom	Vice President Marketing	>5	National/ B2B
8	Management Consulting	United States	Head of Customer Services	>5	National/ B2B
9	Constructions	United Kingdom	Customer Experience Manager	>5	National/ B2B
10	Telecommunications	Luxembourg	Head of Experience Design Team	>5	Global/ B2C
11	Gaming	Sweden	Customer Experience Director	>3	Global/ B2C
12	Hotel	Sweden	COM	>3	National/ B2B
13	Investment Banking	United States	CMO	>3	Global/ B2C
14	Retail	Canada	CEO	>5	Global/ B2C

The companies represented are headquartered in countries with highly developed service sectors (World Bank 2009), such as the United States, Canada, Great Britain, Sweden, Italy, Germany, Luxembourg, and Spain. The sample is consistent with similar inductive, exploratory approaches in which data are collected through interviews using "a judgment sample of persons who can offer some ideas and insights into the phenomenon" (Churchill 1979, p. 67). We achieved data saturation (Glaser & Strauss 1967) after conducting in-depth interviews (each lasting 30–90 minutes) with 14 managers, exceeding the recommended interview number for this research design. Data saturation refers to the point at which no new information or themes are observed in the data (Glaser 2002). We followed the approach suggested by Eisenhardt (1998) which includes the following: (1) selecting case companies and informants in them; (2) gathering, coding and analyzing data using constant comparative analysis; (3) enfolding the literature; and (4) research closure, which may include defining a construct and developing a conceptualization, such as a typology. The interviewees were recruited from the existing networks of the primary research team (Klaus et al. 2012) and were not offered compensation for participation. The interviews were conducted by all three researchers and recorded. The interviews took place via telephone or face to face in the interviewees' offices, according to the personal preference of the individual interviewees. The participants and the organizations they belong to are anonymized because of the confidential nature of the information shared in the interviews.

We adopted Silvestro et al.'s (1992) service classification scheme (Auzair & Langfield-Smith 2005) to identify CX practices that are common across all firms. To ensure cross-validation (Guenzi & Georges 2010), we chose service firms from three archetypes: professional services (such as management consultancies, corporate banks, and investment banks); mass services (such as telecommunications, gaming, and fuel stations); and service shops (such as retail, hotel, retail banking, airlines). The typology covers all possible scenarios and firm constellations, including:

- Equipment-focused to people-focused offerings, depending on whether certain types of equipment (e.g., telecommunication) or contact staff (consultancy) are the core element of the offering;

- Low-contact interaction time (e.g., a few minutes online) to weeks and months of customer contact (e.g., wealth management);
- Low-degree (standard) to high-degree (tailored) customization;
- The degree of discretion, ranging from high discretion, where customer-facing personnel can exercise a high degree of autonomy to decide upon the customer's case, to low discretion, where no decision can be made without a superior's sign-off;
- The ratio of front-office employees to back-office heavy operations employees;
- Product-oriented (emphasis on what the customers buys) versus process-oriented (emphasis on how the offering is delivered) firms.

Table 2.1 includes a detailed profile of the sample.

Data analysis and dimension generation

The interviews were transcribed and coded with NVivo 8.0, which allows researchers to reflect on key themes and codes, and compare data (Di Gregorio 2000). Coding, that is, making sense of the vast amount of data from the interviews, followed the grounded approach described by Ryan and Bernard (2003), which draws heavily from Strauss and Corbin (1990). The grounded approach operates almost in a reverse fashion from traditional social science research. Rather than beginning with a hypothesis, the first step is data collection, using a variety of methods. From the data collected, the key points are marked with a series of *codes*, which are extracted from the text. The codes are grouped into similar *concepts* in order to make the data more workable. From these concepts, *categories* are formed, which are the basis for the creation of the typology. This contradicts the traditional model of research, where the researcher chooses a theoretical framework, and then applies this model to the phenomenon to be studied. In the first step, all attributes, statements with a certain meaning, are identified. The initial categorization of attributes was the outcome of an extended workshop involving the researchers. Each attribute was named and defined. Subsequently, the researchers discussed differences in their attribute categorizations and agreed on revised attributes and category definitions. Some constructs appeared in more than one interview. Each researcher examined transcriptions and individual codes to identify repetitions, and defined standardized construct names, resulting in a coherent coding structure. The analysis generated a pool of 47 attributes in five dimensions of CX strategy and management.

To maximize the face and construct validity of the attributes and dimensions, a panel of expert judges reviewed the attribute pool and generated their own dimensions (Dagger et al. 2007). The panel comprised six marketing academics familiar with CX strategy and practice. First, the panel commented on the clarity, conciseness, and labeling of the attributes and dimensions, and, if necessary, defined their own labels for the attributes. The panel members were asked about similarity of attributes, clarity of phrasing, and terms used in the categorization. In subsequent sessions, the judges were given all of the possible names and descriptions for the individual attributes, together with the original quotes used to label the attributes. The judges were then asked to choose the one that best fit the name and description of the attribute. The research team then compared the findings and selected the names and descriptions emerging from the judges' feedback. In order to qualify, a name or description for an attribute had to be selected by at least five of the six judges.

After agreeing upon the attribute's description, each attribute in the initial pool was printed on an index card and each panel member was asked to create dimensions and sub-dimensions based on the similarity of the attributes of the customer experience. It was up to the members to decide the number of dimensions they used and find appropriate labels and descriptions of the dimensions (Klaus et al. 2013). The sorting procedure resulted in the generation of five dimensions. Next, the attributes of each dimension were sorted into one of seven categories that ranged from "not at all representative" to "strongly representative." Attribute purification began with the exclusion of any attribute rated by the panel members as either "not at all" or only "somewhat" representative. Four members of the panel had to assess the attribute to be "rather" or "strongly" representative for an attribute to be included in the final categorization. Finally, the panel was provided with conceptual descriptions of the resulting five dimensions and asked to assess them as "very applicable," "somewhat applicable," or "not applicable." An attribute needed a minimum assessment of "somewhat applicable" to be retained. This procedure resulted in the retention of all 47 attributes in five dimensions. Five CX managers confirmed the conceptual model and reviewed both the readability and applicability of the five dimensions and corresponding attributes. The next chapter will present the five dimensions of CX management.

chapter 3

The 5 Dimensions of CX Management

Through the process described in Chapter 2, we identified the five dimensions of CX practice as:

1. the definition of CX, its scope and objectives;
2. the management of CX within the firm – processes and implementation;
3. the governance of CX – metrics and leadership;
4. how CX policy is developed over time; and
5. the CX challenges faced by the firm as it looks towards the future.

In this chapter, rather than simply describing the findings of our study, I enrich the presentation with quotes from the managers on how they define their practices, achievements, and challenges.

CX definitions, scope, and objectives

Managers report a wide range of reasons and objectives for initiating their CX programs. Only three of the interviewees, however, articulated a precise definition for their CX strategy/program. Only two managers could identify measurable targets for their CX management. Most of the informants described CX in very broad and ambitious terms, which we felt were somewhat vague. For example, four managers expressed the opinion that customers' expectations of services and value were increasing all the time, and that this trend led them to feel that they had to keep up with their competitors – they regard experience as being a new front in competition in their industry. However, these managers offered very little insight into why this is the case and/or why this is particularly true in their industry. The managers' assertion was often supported by anecdotes of extremely positive or negative customer experiences, which enabled them to lay out the case for improvement in a heuristic way. The managers defined their heuristic approach as experience-based techniques for problem-solving and learning, leading to discoveries and subsequent solutions which are not guaranteed to be optimal – a "learning-by-doing" approach. A manager from a major bank said that his organization began focusing on CX when it encountered high rates of customer defection, despite enjoying higher levels in measures of customer satisfaction than its competitors.

> We basically lost clients despite our high customer satisfaction rating. So, we know that there were other reasons why clients were leaving us. (Respondent 5)

This phenomenon was a reoccurring theme and one of the triggers for managers' realization that certain measurements aren't sufficient to explain or predict consumer behavior nowadays. Three managers presented the narrative from a more proactive perspective, suggesting that the objective of their programs was to enhance their firm's competitiveness (performance) through innovation and differentiation.

> We will use our customer experience program to deliver the best experiences for the ever-increasing expectations of our customers, and, of course, beat our competitors to the punch. (Respondent 14)

Regardless of whether the motivation is to respond to customer expectations or a desire to excel, the mechanisms connecting CX management to outcomes, the intermediary between cause and effect, were branding and customer service. Nearly all managers felt that a high-quality customer experience reinforces a brand by delivering its core benefits and values coherently across various, not necessary all, customer touch-points and channels. The vast majority of managers also believe that high-quality customer experiences would increase customer commitment to a brand and generate recommendations through improved service quality. These managers believed that, even if they couldn't measure the reasons why consumers give recommendations, they could at least use one benchmark, the Net Promoter Score (NPS), to see an outcome of their efforts. A prominent thread throughout the interviews was that the goal of the firms' CX management is to ensure better delivery of compelling brand promises, thereby enhancing both emotional attachment to the brand and service quality, a combination that, in the managers' opinion, generates loyalty and recommendation. Again, though, managers could not generate any hard evidence for these relationships. Managers simply *believe*, because it sounds both reasonable and logical.

Most of the interviewees struggled to articulate either a concise expression of CX, or a well-defined scope for their programs. Definitions were typically broad and related to customer points of contact. Customer experience and CX management were often described as "holistic" and expressed through storytelling instead of a salient set of strategies, tactics, processes, and tools:

customer experience and CX management were often described as "holistic"

> *Well, there is not an established definition, but we tend [to use] the sum of all interactions that customers have of our brand. (Respondent 4)*

> *I think it is a holistic question, as I said before. You can involve all the actions in the process, not only the airline, but also the airport, security measures, the airport access, the access to the downtown. It is a holistic process. We have to understand the reason of the trip and the way you can add value in the process. (Respondent 1)*

Sometimes, experience management is defined in the context of peer-level interaction and engagement. For example, the manager of a conference center defined CX management at the level of each event attendee he hosts:

> *Our ambition is to make sure that every individual in the group has a positive experience. (Respondent 12)*

There was a range of opinions as to how, if at all, involved with the firm customers want to be. Two managers concluded that services should be ubiquitous, smooth, and unobtrusive, and that customers should not be aware of the provider. A telecommunication manager manifested this view by stating that the best service is if the customers do not even perceive it. This utilitarian perspective is contrasted by the research on immersive experiences, in which the firms provide stimuli to multiple senses in order to engage with consumers on different levels. Most of the interviewees were in businesses that suggest a middle ground, with CX a means of embedding an emotional attachment to a service function:

> *The opportunity for building the relationship is there when your customers truly value the idea of getting help that goes beyond speed and fulfillment. It is about understanding and caring and those things. (Respondent 9)*

There was a clearer identification as to what constitutes a poor customer experience: a lack of integration in the firm's message or after-sales service across the firm's channels (touch-points); indifferent or unhelpful front-office personnel; and/or an inflexible, impersonalized experience because of rigidly enforced service agreements. Therefore, the departure point of most organizations' CX programs was the integration of their organization's activities across all channels to provide a consistently good experience as defined by the customer. Whereas Total Quality Management (TQM) and service quality start from a statistical analysis of process performance, CX management focuses on customer assessment of an overall experience, an experience that is both emotional and branded. Managers talked about an "outside-in" rather than "inside-out" process design:

> *The single idea [was] that we should look at the experience from the eyes of the customer. (Respondent 6)*

The integration of the firm's front and back offices was featured in eight of the interviews. Managers defined this integration as customer-facing employees having an appropriate level of customer data coupled with perfect visibility of end-to-end service delivery processes. This, ideally, leads to a scenario where their firm can serve both their existing and potential customers well. Firms with a well-defined customer service strategy extend their front and back office integration to include their suppliers. This is particularly true for firms where the performance of suppliers is visible to customers. Just think about industries for which outsourcing (part of the customer experience) has always been an option, such as retailing and manufacturing, and industries such as the following, which are now starting to develop aggressive long-term outsourcing strategies caused by dramatic shifts: entertainment, media, and publishing (affected by new distribution and business models, e.g., the impact of Web 2.0); software and hi-tech businesses (affected, for example, by the impact of cloud-computing, rapid commoditization of products, low-cost providers etc.); financial services (affected by re-regulation and compliance measures etc.).

The importance of a consistent customer experience over time and across channels reflects the origins of customer management in TQM, and managers used terms from TQM when discussing the reliability of customers' experiences with their firms. Five interviewees described how CX management programs emerged from service quality and customer satisfaction initiatives. These initiatives demonstrated a need for greater company integration, a focus on satisfaction, loyalty, and improving positive recommendations.

> We kicked off [customer experience] about ten years ago (in) an initiative we called "Perfect Delivery," which was all about getting the product right [...] free from any known defect [...] We've also asked our clients [which] key objective they would like us to achieve. [When we started] [...] we weren't great and we wanted to be world class, and the company is now known as a quality organization [...] Our vision is 100 percent recommendations, supported by making the product perfect and the process simple and the people engaging. (Respondent 9)

In addition to process control and integration, CX programs show an explicit concern with the training and development of their customer-facing employees to deliver consistent high-quality service. Almost all of the interviewees acknowledged that their employees are the most crucial deliverers of customer experiences. One described the challenges of working across many functions (organization development, brand marketing and customer service) to implement the human resources policies required by the CX program. In three cases, we found that people development was a resource constraint in advancing CX management practices.

Management of customer experience

The central thread of CX management is the creation and enhancement of a common customer experience across all touch-points through process and people development.

Process development

For five companies, the CX development process commenced with touch-point mapping that identified the critical moments where CX was enhanced or degraded. Subsequently, process re-engineering was carried out to integrate the channels. The process was almost always supported by outside consultants who used their own process-mapping tools and methods. The managers revealed that their initial work, like TQM before it, focused excessively on developing better processes and was insufficiently guided by insight into customers' assessment of the experiences. Most managers we interviewed had come to this realization during the early stages of developing their CX program and had taken corrective actions.

People development

There was widespread recognition of the need to ensure that the behavior of customer-facing employees met the expectations of the CX program. Indeed, a manager from the hotel sector specifically mentioned the Service Profit Chain (SPC) (Heskett et al. 1997) when relating the role of employees to profitable outcomes. The SPC concept posits that firm profit and growth are stimulated primarily by customer loyalty. Loyalty is seen as a direct outcome of (high) customer satisfaction. Satisfaction is fundamentally induced by the value of services provided to customers. Happy, dedicated, and productive employees create value. Employee satisfaction, in turn, results primarily from high-quality support services and policies that enable employees to deliver results to customers. Thus, according to the SPC, happy employees will ultimately drive the firm's growth.

People programs include extensive communication to encourage customer-facing employees to become self-reflective practitioners, thus improving their ability to continuously deliver the values underlying their brand, as defined by the firm. There is recognition that CX requires more from employees than strict adherence to standardized business processes and rules. The concept is hard to define and employees are required to think beyond the fulfillment of tasks to help customers achieve their desired outcomes and support the emotional aspect of experience that bonds customers with a brand. This is not an easy task at all, as almost all managers agreed upon. This shift in employee focus is noticeable in business services where CX and the development of key customer-facing managers are tightly linked:

> We let people try to make their own mistakes. We guide [them] through best practice [...] we take a group of site managers around other people's sites and say "Have a look" [...] I think that's a much better way to get into people's heads than, let's say, someone dictating to them and say "Do this." (Respondent 12)

Therefore, attracting, managing, and developing people who can create great customer experiences is a major theme in most of the interviews.

Some firms had changed their approach to hiring by recruiting employees for their emotional maturity and for personal values supportive of the CX strategy and program:

> We much more hire on attitudes [...] do their core values match up to our core values? What's their mindset towards the clients? (Respondent 12)

Beyond influencing recruitment criteria, CX programs guide staff training. There are a range of mechanisms revealed in the interviews, including mentoring and communication; one respondent even talked about a staff academy where CX is a major part of the "curriculum." Most managers describe people development as a gradual and interactive process where new recruits are given time and support to absorb new working practices and perceptions. However, there is evidence that those with well-established CX management programs extend this development process to their suppliers' employees. Based on evidence, albeit limited, we suggest that extending CX management skills development to the firm's broader network is a "second-wave" CX management practice. Such practice is consistent with research from supply chain management and the co-creation of value literature (Vargo & Lusch 2004).

Rewards clearly matched CX objectives; those with well-developed programs reward customer-facing people using a combination of financial targets (e.g., sales, profit), service quality measures (e.g., on-time, right first time), and customer assessments of the experience. Three managers discussed the challenge of identifying and then rewarding individuals' "good" behavior. When people development extends to suppliers, the focal firm assesses and rewards them against measures of CX. In the firm demonstrating the most developed practice in this area, the firm and its suppliers have developed a more open and trusting relationship, revolving around and remunerated through how their customers perceive their individual experience.

Since individual rewards can be difficult to implement, one manager described how he was building a community of practice to identify and embed good CX delivery. This firm accumulates and synthesizes learning from its CX program, and publishes it to customer-facing employees. A conference center manager identified a perhaps more "low-tech" approach in holding regular group meetings with employees:

> *If something has occurred, we try to sit down as soon as possible to have a meeting to discuss what happened, how it happened, what we did. During this everyone gets a chance to give some feedback. (Respondent 3)*

Governance of customer experience

Despite the variation in scope and definition, the way CX programs are governed is consistent across much of the sample. Of the 14 companies,

11 measured customer experience through surveys, and 6 of the 11 used NPS (Reichheld 2006), though the same managers expressed dissatisfaction with that metric.

> *I'm very skeptical [...] It's reactive rather than proactive, and you can measure the history but you won't tell anything about what you're going to do [...] it's very hard to come down to a specific number or anything like that. (Respondent 4)*

Managers suggested that boards of directors appreciate the simplicity of NPS but are not convinced that it is more informative than the customer satisfaction results used previously. Most employed a battery of measurements and research instruments to guide the program and to act with what they described as "the voice of the customer." These instruments ranged from a mixture of other scores (e.g., customer satisfaction, level of complaints), general customer and brand surveys, focus groups, and anecdotal evidence from customers.

> *We are aware that customer experience goes beyond quality of service, that is why we try to be up to date with all the tendencies and all the academic research [... and] add all the [relevant] metrics to our research. (Respondent 2)*

Surveys remained a core method of assessing customer experience and both setting and reinforcing the CX agenda. Most firms modified existing customer surveys to include what they believed captured experiential elements of marketing strategy.

> *We've redesigned (our) questionnaires to focus much more on the experience rather than the (operational elements). (Respondent 9)*

One firm interviews hundreds of consumers each week, globally and on a non-representative sampling basis. The latter is designed as an early warning system. Another firm correlated unprofitable projects with poor customer experience scores on its customer satisfaction survey. This clear association with performance built support for its CX program internally. A contrary anecdote came from a bank that found it difficult to articulate the value of customer experience, which hindered it when developing its CX program.

> It was difficult to come up with a single platform to put all the information, the input, together [into] metrics and then weight them in terms of importance or relevance for [the] customer [...] So we found ourselves in a situation with lots of input and information but without any solid framework or system to put them into a map or to manage properly. (Respondent 6)

The interviews conveyed an almost emotional or sentimental quality about the idea that customers are promoting the firm. NPS seemed to evoke greater top management support than traditional measures of customer assessment.

> I think that [the net] promoter is usually driven by senior management whereas customer satisfaction usually is driven by marketing. I think where it's driven from marketing, it doesn't [work] and that is [...] the history of [...] 15 years of customer satisfaction programs. (Respondent 7)

Ten managers commented on the commitment of top management to CX, and, not surprisingly, all felt it was essential.

CX policy development

Responsibility for CX management programs varied. In three organizations, senior managers nominated themselves as program champions. In four others, the program leader held a middle management position.

The extent to which CX program managers felt their efforts were supported varied enormously. As one manager stated, the project started from marketing and research but the team soon realized that CX required change across the organization. Regrettably, they were unable to marshal sufficient support from top management. The firm did not establish performance outcome measurements, and we observed a link between a well-articulated set of objectives and senior management support of CX.

Research, customer satisfaction, and marketing communication were seen as both key catalysts of CX management and a means of providing the voice of the customer. For a European bank, CX began as a marketing initiative, arising from a research project on improving customer service and communication, but it evolved slowly from that core. When experience management originates out of concern for performance or the quality of customer relationships, it is able to garner top management support immediately and diffuses rapidly across the organization. For some, keeping experience management within the confines of marketing proves to be problematic. Irrespective of its origins, research retains an essential role as the voice of the customer and a benchmark of progress.

> The whole experience design [team] is the voice of the users [and] we are in constant battle [with] the business. (Respondent 10)

There is evidence that formal quality improvement programs can act as a catalyst for CX investment. In a construction firm, a "perfect delivery" initiative was the starting point for what became an extensive CX program.

CX challenges

There is more consensus on the challenges of CX implementation than there is on its definition, scope or management. Three main challenges emerged from the data: (1) managing the multi-faceted nature of CX in an integrated and coherent manner; (2) linking CX to financial outcomes; and (3) the need to view CX strategy as a long-term commitment.

Managing the multi-faceted nature of CX

Results suggest that organizations struggle to understand what constitutes CX, describing it as a sum of all interactions between the client and the company. Two organizations held a more sophisticated and complete view of the stages of the overall customer experience:

> I think it is a holistic question as you said before. You can involve all the actions in the process, not only the airline, but also the airport, security

measures, the airport access, the access to the downtown. It is a holistic process. We have to understand the reason of the trip and the way you can add value in the process. (Respondent 1)

Even managers from organizations committed to CX reported difficulty with implementing strategies across functions:

Different business functions seldom speak to each other, so you end up with this functionality [split] between human resources, marketing and operations, each targeted on the performance of their own individual results rather than the context of the whole. (Respondent 8)

Others were simply overwhelmed, asserting that they

[…] were not able to analyze or to find a way to weight all these inputs and suggestions and complaints sometimes and put them into an operational roadmap of how to tackle, what to tackle first, and how? (Respondent 7)

Nonetheless, the majority were optimistic that they would overcome such issues.

[…] someday in the future we're going to have to put all this together and have a more integrated view of how things should be dealt with from a customer experience point of view. (Respondent 3)

Measuring the link between CX and financial outcomes

There was no coherent view on the most appropriate measures. Eight firms were unable to quantify the relationship between their CX programs and financial outcomes. Respondents often referred to a causal chain between better customer experiences, improved satisfaction, and then increased loyalty. Others tried to estimate the direct impact of their investments in CX on their revenue or profits. No clear evidence for the measurability of this direct link was provided, which reflects the first challenge of CX strategy, or as one respondent suggested:

If I can't clearly define it, how can I know if it's going to improve (our performance)? (Respondent 2)

CX as a long-term investment

Even if organizations overcome this challenge, they face an uphill battle to create the awareness that investments in CX do not provide immediate and recognizable financial outcomes. The consensus is that while a reasonably long-term view of the strategy is necessary, there are pressures to demonstrate immediate return:

> […] building it (the CX program) conflicts with short-term goals, aims, and priorities of shareholders and so on. (Respondent 13)

The corresponding five CX management practices and their descriptions are summarized in Table 3.1.

After carefully analysing all case studies according to the five dimensions of CX practice, we developed an even more detailed view of what the 47 "key ingredients" of each of the five dimensions are, and created Table 3.2 to demonstrate our coding approach.

Having established the five main dimensions of CX strategy and management practice, we are now able to build a typology of how the companies managed their CX program and explore the crucial relationship between these practices and profitability.

TABLE 3.1   Customer experience management dimensions

Dimensions	Definition
CX definitions, scope, and objectives	Organizations' definitions of CX, its scope, and objectives
Governance of CX	Comments related to a need for systematic management of CX under leadership of a responsible manager
Management of CX	Reports a model of ideal experiences and a set of business processes against that ideal (i.e., existence of a CX business plan/model and business processes)
CX policy development	Describes the instigating force behind introduction of a CX program, and how objectives were formulated
CX challenges	Describes key management challenges that organizations face in CX practice

TABLE 3.2 Customer experience dimensions and attributes

	CX definitions, scope, and objectives
1	KSO – CX as key strategy/objectives
2	OOS – Origins of CX strategy based on importance of CX for businesses/origins
3	MCI – CX strategy as tool for multi-channel integration
4	LCL – Linking CX to customer loyalty
5	LCS – Linking CX to customer satisfaction
6	LCR – Linking CX to customer recommendations
7	ESQ – CX as enhanced service quality
8	DFO – CX as a differentiator for organizations
9	IDO – CX as innovation driver for organizations
10	HEC – Historical evolution of CX throughout the entire organization
11	BEN – CX as brand reinforcement
12	ITP – CX strategy as integrator of all touch-points
13	DOP – CX definition from organizational point-of-view
14	EPN – Example(s) of positive/negative CX
15	IOE – Importance of emotions in CX
16	INV – Invisible CX
17	EXT – Extraordinary experiences
18	CPO – CX from customers' point of view
19	ITO – Who/what introduced CX to the organization?
20	PAC – People- and culture-related
	Governance of customer experience
21	PSM – Purposeful, systematic CX management versus outcomes and aims
22	RMD – Responsible management for definition and control of CX
23	IOM – Importance of measurements for delivering CX
24	CXB – Customer experience as brand enhancer
25	RVP – Reactive versus proactive measurements of CX
26	SAM – Sophisticated approaches to measure CX
27	DIF – Diffusion
	Management of customer experience
28	CFP – Connection to customer-facing people's service delivery
29	TAI – Training and instruction for customer-facing employees
30	PRD – CX as people recruitment and development tool – human capital management

(continued)

TABLE 3.2 Continued

31	ICMR – Individuals' contributions to CX are measured and rewarded
32	BOI – Back-office integration in CX delivery
33	EOE – Expected outcomes for employees
34	EOO – Expected outcomes for organization and shareholders
35	ICFT – Integration of cross-functional teams for CX delivery and management
36	DMA – CX delivery manual
37	EOC – Expected outcomes for customers
	CX policy development
38	BMBP – CX business model/business plan
39	HOF – How were CX objectives formulated?
40	BPRO – CX business processes
41	ICLE – Importance of C-level executive support/sponsoring for the success of the CX initiative
	CX challenges
42	SUCH – CX supply chain
43	LCXFO – Linking CX to financial outcomes
44	HOLN – Holistic nature of CX
45	CSPN – Context-specific nature of CX
46	CXLTC – CX as long-term commitment
47	IETPD – Integration of all touch-points for CX delivery

The 3 Types of CX Management Practice

Generating the typology

In order to produce a typology of CX practice, we use the CX strategy and management dimensions we explored and established in the last chapter. Our primary research team, consisting of some of the leading marketing researchers, scrutinized each of the 14 CX case studies and interviews individually, according to the five dimensions of CX practice. In order to do this, we converted the key ingredients of each dimension in a corresponding statement (see Table 3.2).

The corresponding statements read as follows:

BEN – *We manage our customer experience as a means of reinforcing our brand's values.*

BMBP – *We have a definite business model for customer experience management that defines the concept, its purpose, expected outcomes, and the resources it will receive.*

BOI – *Linking customer-facing employees with back-office or operational systems is vital to delivering excellent customer experience.*

BPRO – *Customer experience practices are supported by systematic analysis that assesses customers' expectations, the experience delivered at all points of customer contact, and the effectiveness of the processes we deploy to deliver customer experience.*

CXB – *Customer experience is an essential part of our brand.*

CXLTC – *We accept that customer experience requires long-term commitment and manage accordingly.*

CFP – *Customer-facing people are the focal point of our customer experience program.*

CPO – *The expectations of our customers are a key building block of our customer experience strategy and practice.*

CSPN – *We acknowledge that excellent customer experience will change by market, location and other contextual factors.*

DFO – *Customer experience is a significant differentiator for us in the market.*

DIF – *Back-office and customer-facing employees are fully aware of customer experience objectives and the progress towards them that we are making.*

DMA – *We document best practice in customer experience for training and development purposes.*

DOP – *We have a well-defined process for managing customer experience and monitoring its impact upon our business performance.*

EOC – *Our customer experience strategy is developed in consideration of outcomes relevant to our customers.*

EOE – *Our customer experience strategy is developed in consideration of employees' outcomes.*

EOO – *Our customer experience strategy is developed in consideration of our overall organizational strategy and shareholder expectations.*

EPN – *We can identify many incidents where good or bad customer experience impacted our business.*

ESQ – *We believe that customer experience is based primarily on the quality of our service.*

EXT – *Excellent customer experience involves doing something extra and unanticipated.*

HEC – *Customer experience started out as a (pilot) project and has now a major impact on our strategy and the way we do business.*

HOF – *Customer experience strategy and objectives are developed through formal and transparent strategy and planning processes.*

HOLN – *Accepting that the holistic nature of customer experience makes it hard to define, we nonetheless work hard to classify customer experience, set boundaries for it and identify measurable outcomes.*

ICFT – *Customer experience management forces us to integrate functions and business units across the organization.*

ICLE – *The customer experience strategy and program enjoy strong and visible support from the most senior managers of the firm.*

ICMR – *We assess the individual employee's contribution to customer experience and link this to his/her rewards.*

IDO – *We embarked on a customer experience program as a means of addressing emerging customer demands.*

IETPD – *We create a consistent customer experience across all customer touch-points.*

INV – *We believe that the best service is the service that the customer does not recognize at all.*

IOE – *Providing an excellent customer experience creates a strong emotional bond between our customers and us.*

IOM – *We have a well-defined means of measuring customer experience and report on its progress regularly.*

ITO – *We are well aware of who/or what event started our customer experience program.*

ITP – *We are confident that we provide a consistent customer experience across all points of customer contact.*

KSO – *Customer experience is a key strategic objective for the entire organization, and we manage and measure its impact on business performance.*

LCXFO – *Accepting that it is difficult to link customer experience management to specific financial outcomes, we nonetheless strive to do so and are making good progress.*

LCL – *We have well-defined measures of how customer experience impacts customer loyalty.*

LCR – *We have well-defined measures of how customer experience impacts customer recommendations (word of mouth).*

LCS – *We have well-defined measures of how customer experience impacts customer satisfaction.*

MCI – *Managing customer experience has made us integrate our various channels to market better.*

OOS – *Improving customer experience has enhanced our competitiveness.*

PAC – *Central to our customer experience program is to ensure that all our people act commensurate with our brand and values when dealing with customers.*

PRD – *Employee's contribution to customer experience forms an important part of our HR management: training, recruitment, and rewards.*

PSM – *Customer experience is a recognized management activity linked to measurable outcomes.*

RMD – *Everyone in the organization knows who (or which group) is responsible for managing customer experience, reporting on its outcomes, and developing its practices.*

RVP – *Existing measurements of our customer experience delivery are discussed, their limitations are acknowledged, and we are working to improve our measurement of customer experience.*

SAM – *We measure customer experience on a broader basis than net promoter score alone.*

SUCH – *Supply chain management is an integral component of our customer experience strategy and management because it is critical to delivery of excellent customer experience.*

TAI – *We train and develop our customer-facing employees how to deliver excellent customer experience.*

The three primary and two additional researchers familiar with the research domain and objectives assessed each statement on a scale of 0–10, anchored at one end by "there is no evidence to support the statement," and at the other by "there is explicit evidence to support the statement." This numerical assessment serves as support and evidence of each statement for each individual case. Next, the primary researchers agreed upon a final value for each statement in order to assess each respondent's description and facilitate a more unconcealed and transparent form of cross-case analysis. The proportion of agreement among the primary researchers on their scoring of each statement was high, demonstrating the high reliability and agreement of their individual findings. We measured the level of agreement using the Spearman correlation coefficient between researchers, which was very strong with $r = 0.88$, $p < 0.05$. We summed up the values for each dimension of each company (case) so that we could assign a value for every single one of the practices the firms displayed. This was helpful as the subsequent generation of the three types of practice demonstrated differences across each dimension.

Each case study was again scrutinized across the practices displayed within each of the five dimensions, as well as on an overall basis. On the basis of judgment, discussion, and prior research recommendations, the primary research team generated three groupings, which were subsequently labeled "Preservers," "Transformers," and "Vanguards." Table 4.1 illustrates the summary of our findings and cluster allocation. We combined this information with what we feel are some representative attributes and their aggregates (see Table 4.2).

TABLE 4.1   Customer experience practice typology

	Typology		
	Preservers	**Transformers**	**Vanguards**
Definition, Scope and Objectives	Extension of service.	Acknowledge the broad nature of CE and its strategic importance.	Broad and strategic. No other priority "tops" it.
Governance	Functional level and initiatives. Focus within the firm.	Link CE to organizational goals and strategy.	Policy and operational levels aligned. Continual assessment and improvement.
Management (Operational)	Service quality, channel integration.	Focus on channel integration, customer loyalty, brand perception, and recommendations.	Integration of business processes through the supply chain and across channels. Commensurate HR and Organizational Development policies.

(continued)

TABLE 4.1 Continued

	Typology		
	Preservers	**Transformers**	**Vanguards**
Policy Development	Lack of overarching vision.	Strategic intent, which varies as to sponsorship.	Committed top-level sponsorship, cross-functional ownership.
Challenges	Not a strategic initiative, cannot make the business case for change.	Looking for senior sponsorship, more appropriate metrics, business, and process models.	Reinvention, and maintaining competitive edge. Business partners sometimes a limiting factor.

TABLE 4.2 CX dimensions differences between CX practices

CX dimensions (plus cluster score on a scale from 0=little evidence to 10=strong evidence)	Description	Preservers		Transformers	Vanguards
CX definition, scope, and objectives	Organizations' definitions of CX, its scope, and objectives.	Examples: ITP – CX strategy as integrator of all touch-points	3.75	5.33	8.75
		EPN – Example(s) of positive/negative CX	2.75	5.50	7.75
CX governance	Comments related to a need for systematic management of CX under leadership of a responsible manager.	Examples: SAM – Sophisticated approaches to measure CX	4.75	5.00	8.25
		PSM – Purposeful systematic CX management versus outcomes and aims	5.75	5.67	8.50

(continued)

TABLE 4.2 Continued

CX dimensions (plus cluster score on a scale from 0=little evidence to 10=strong evidence)	Description	Preservers		Transformers	Vanguards
CX management (operational)	Reports a model of ideal experiences and a set of business processes against that ideal (i.e. existence of a CX business plan/model and business processes).	Examples: PRD – CX as people recruitment and development tool – human capital management	3.25	5.33	7.75
		BOI – Back-office integration in CX delivery	4.50	7.00	8.25
CX policy development	Describes the instigating force behind introduction of a CX program, and how objectives were formulated.	Examples: BMBP – CX business model/ business plan	2.75	4.17	8.75
		HOF – How were CX objectives formulated?	2.50	4.27	8.25
CX Challenges	Describes key management challenges organizations face in CX practice.	Examples: HOLN – Holistic nature of CX	6.50	6.50	9.00
		IETPD – Integration of all touch- points for CX delivery	3.50	5.17	7.75

Typology

We followed Hambrick's (1984) approach to move from dimensions to a typology as described in the earlier chapters. The inductively derived solution comprises the three CX practices: Preservers, Transformers, and Vanguards. Each is described in more detail below. It is most important to note that these types display differences across all five dimensions of CX practice (see Table 4.1).

Despite discussing CX as a major strategic initiative, our findings suggest that for Preservers its practice is little more than an extension of existing channel or quality processes. Vanguards believe CX practice generates sustained competition, whereas Transformers elevate CX to a strategic level, but have yet to implement it effectively. Our data do not let us determine whether Transformers will ultimately become Vanguards, but *Measuring Customer Experience* will deliver more insight into if and how this can be achieved. Now, let's take a look at these practices, one by one.

Preservers

Preservers define CX management as an extension or development of existing service delivery practices. They assess its effectiveness using traditional measures of service quality or customer satisfaction. While acknowledging its importance, Preservers are incapable of making a strong business case for CX to their top management. Preservers are characterized by a series of limited initiatives rather than the construction of a comprehensive program based on a well-articulated, long-term vision. Their programs lack central control, the development of complementary business processes, and an overarching vision. The inability to connect CX management practice to identifiable goals and outcomes inhibits the development of a compelling business case and the elevation of CX to a strategic level. Interviewees whose firms were Preservers narrated a few examples of positive and negative CX, and had little knowledge of their programs' origins. While acknowledging the importance of accountability, they struggle to develop appropriate measures of CX effectiveness. Their focus is on organizational results, whereas outcomes for employees, customers, and corresponding core business processes are not developed fully. The latter include the integration of customer touch-points and back-office functions. Moreover, Preservers do not provide adequate training for their customer-facing employees responsible for delivering customer experiences; nor do they discuss the role of their business partners in delivering these experiences. Although they acknowledge the importance of CX management, they do not develop the appropriate practices. During the times I had an opportunity to present our typology, the attending audience, when asked to describe these practices in their own terms, offered the following narratives: rebranding exercise; putting lipstick on a pig; window-dressing.

Transformers

Transformers believe that CX is linked positively to financial performance, and acknowledge its holistic nature and the resulting challenges in scoping and defining its management. The results strongly suggest the presence of internal discourse concerning CX strategy and its management practice. Unlike Preservers, Transformers see the contribution of customer-facing personnel as vital. Transformers are convinced that CX influences customer satisfaction, loyalty, recommendations, and brand perception. In contrast to Preservers, who manage CX as an extension of existing practices, Transformers believe CX is strategically important and highlight the necessity of designing and executing a corresponding strategy based on the organization's definition of CX.

Transformers connect CX practice to organizational goals, and link practice to existing measures of customer outcomes. However, Transformers acknowledge the shortcomings of existing measures and search for more sophisticated approaches to assess CX and its performance impact. Transformers articulate a detailed history of their programs, which are often initiated by a top executive. All Transformer organizations have clearly designated particular individuals as being responsible for CX. These individuals do not necessarily constitute a central and cross-departmental team. Transformers acknowledge the impact of customer-facing personnel on delivering CX and influencing customer behavior, and develop appropriate training programs.

In comparison to a Preserver's focus on incremental improvements, Transformers strive to become a CX-focused organization, acknowledging both the broad nature of CX and the implications for managing CX throughout the organization. These organizations accept a long-term commitment to transformation. Nonetheless, they struggle to develop a CX business model and the corresponding business processes, resulting in an emphasis on existing processes. Transformers struggle to link CX to financial outcomes, but are convinced of the positive influence of CX on customer behavior and organizational goals. But if, as Michael Porter argues, to be successful over the long-term a firm must select one single generic strategy, are Preservers in danger of being "stuck in the middle" and therefore unable to achieve a competitive advantage?

Vanguards

Vanguards have a clear strategic model of CX management that affects their entire organization, and they develop matching business processes and practices to ensure its effective implementation. While Transformers merely acknowledge the broad-based challenges of CX management, Vanguards integrate functions and customer touchpoints to ensure that the customer experiences across their own business and those of their partners are consistent. Vanguards use existing measurements to track the impact of their programs based on customer-centric outcomes and evaluations, while constantly developing new tools and practices to support the overall strategy. For example, Vanguards recognize the crucial role of accountability and are constantly improving their measures of the effectiveness and efficiency of CX practice. Vanguards manage the design and measurement of experiences through a central group that integrates multiple organizational functions. CX practice is founded on the conviction that satisfying expected outcomes for customers is the driver of organizational performance. Training, recruitment, and human resources development are guided by the CX strategy. Thus, employees are rewarded for delivering experiences that customers value. In Vanguard organizations, management receives clear and visible support from top executives. Practice continually develops the CX business model based upon research and is implemented across all business functions. Vanguard organizations measure customer satisfaction and loyalty to use as evidence for monitoring and assessing the effectiveness of the CX strategy.

In summary, unsurprisingly, we find a variety of CX management practices. While scholars have been developing conceptual models for CX, and identifying its antecedents and consequences for some time, the concept itself has only recently been popularized and adopted in companies as a management strategy. Researchers, managers, and consultants have yet to agree on a definition of CX, and based upon the evidence it is fair to assess CX practice as emergent rather than established.

Though sometimes inconsistent, managerial definitions and the scope of CX reflect what we find in academic literature. The dominant themes emerging from our interviews are that CX management enacts the firm's brand values and provides emotional and functional benefits to customers through motivated employees and consistently across various customer touch-points and channels. The notion of a sequence of encounters with customers designed by the firm and leading to an emotional attachment to the brand is also a central theme in research (Hume et al. 2006); the centrality of people in CX is equally well documented (e.g., Heskett et al. 1997).

Analyzing what managers do in practice, the typology suggests CX management is a development of both quality and relationship marketing practices. Managers articulate clearly the origins of their CX programs from existent activities in one or both areas. Typically, a firm identifies poor quality and/or inconsistent service delivery as an inhibitor to attracting and retaining their most profitable customers, and envisions a CX program to address the issues. Managers, without exception, take a pragmatic perspective, and position CX as an extension of well-understood, existing activities.

While the "what" of CX management is aligned broadly with scientific research findings, the "how" diverges. Researchers' advice for implementing CX involves deploying process management tools around a sequence of customer encounters and extending those tools to design elements that provoke emotional responses. Accepting that traditional quality management focuses too narrowly on the repeatability of service actions within a tight variance of output, CX scholars create tools that focus on functional and emotional outcomes including the Servicescape (Bitner 1992), multi-level service design (Patricio et al. 2011), and learning from drama (Goodwin et al. 1996). We found evidence for the use of process-based tools in only one interview. The dominant management activities associated with CX were channel (touch-point) integration and back–front office integration. An implicit assumption held by the managers was that delivering their brand values consistently will improve CX. This approach confuses consistency with effectiveness. The relationship between the consistent delivery of brand values and the creation of customer value, and/or business outcomes, is, if existent, only indirect.

Eschewing calls in the literature for measuring the CX construct (Verhoef et al. 2009; Klaus & Maklan 2012), managers use customer satisfaction and NPS to monitor customers' overall assessments of encounters with the firm. While consistent with the broader definition of CX, neither NPS nor satisfaction generates the forensic data to identify those areas of experience that influence experience the most. Equally, such measures limit the universe to existing customers and fail to identify the experiences of lapsed and competitive users, who are normally the majority of the market. Managers often recognize the limitations of their CX measurement policies but either do not know of a better measure or feel that the simplicity of a single number (satisfaction or NPS) outweighs the benefits of accuracy.

Our findings also challenge a widely held view in the literature that CX practices are context specific. We find common practices, and moreover, common challenges, across all contexts. This seems to hold across B2B and B2C. Similar to Lemke et al. (2011), we found only limited differences between the practices of B2B and B2C organizations. Whilst the business customer is often described as a multi-agent decision-making unit (Webster Jr. & Wind 1972; Johnston & Bonoma 1981; McDonald et al. 1997), respondents talked about them in the singular. They perceive a client experience as the sum of all experiences across all agents of that decision unit. Hence, managerial practices correspond with those found in B2C companies across all three types.

The primary hurdles firms must overcome to develop a coherent CX management strategy are: (1) defining what is or what constitutes CX; (2) demonstrating its link to performance; (3) establishing a clear governance structure for CX policy and continual improvement; (4) creating a CX program; (5) training the staff involved in it. We find substantial evidence that the primary challenges to developing and implementing a CX strategy are based on the lack of a clear definition of what constitutes CX and how to measure it. Despite the lack of definition and being driven by belief rather than evidence, CX is a, if not *the*, strategic objective for organizations.

Let's reflect for a moment … We now know lots about the history of CX, its origins, and how to avoid possible traps. Based upon this we explored how CX is managed in the real world, and discovered that there are three distinctive practices, those of Preservers, Transformers, and Vanguards, which are common across industries, segments, location, and company size. So, how can we use this knowledge to our benefit? Well, first, we have to establish whether one of the three practices is more profitable, and the next chapter is dedicated to answering this question.

5

Linking CX Practices to Profitability

Researchers, managers, and consultants alike champion the notion that optimizing the customer experience is the key strategy for generating enhanced sales revenues, market share, and profitability. However, until now, there was no typology to assist us in the task of putting this notion to the test and establishing which strategies are the most profitable ones.

In order to achieve this, we conducted a global study, conducting interviews with 311 CX managers around the globe. The interviewers asked managers to rank their agreement on a 7-point scale for all 48 CX management practice items in order to determine which cluster (Preservers, Transformers, Vanguards) their practices belonged to. In addition, managers answered various business, personal, demographic, firm performance, and behavioral questions. We analyzed the data using the SPSS and Latent Gold software packages to ensure the validity and reliability of our findings.

Who shared their insights – information about our experts

The majority of respondents were experienced managers. Respondents' ages were mainly above 29 (46%) and 46 years (43.4%), and their work history with their firm spanned at least 3–5 years (58.2%) or more (41.8%). Almost two-thirds of respondents held more senior positions. To be more precise, 35.4 percent held CEO or Director/Executive positions and another 36.7 percent were in managerial positions. Less than a third (27.9%) held "other" positions. The firms' headquarters were in the United States (32.2%), the United Kingdom (19. 9%), Australia (18%), and Canada (17.7%). Only 12.2 percent of firms had headquarters in other countries (e.g., Finland, Sweden, and Norway). Firms were mainly significant in size, with the number of employees ranging between 21 and 500 (34.4%) or over 500 (44.1%). We achieved an excellent split between new firms being operational for up to five years (49.8%) and the remaining firms being well established.

The sample was evenly split between firms' offerings and the markets they served. Approximately half (49.5%) of all respondents' firms were service providers; the other half classified themselves as product/manufacturing firms. Of the service firms, 44 percent of all those surveyed provided services to businesses (B2B), while 56 percent offered services to consumers' markets (B2C). The ratio was similar in the product/manufacturing category, where half provided goods to businesses (54%) and the remaining 46 percent provide goods to consumer markets (see Table 5.1).

Firms' activities

Customer experience was relevant to all the firms we surveyed (see Table 5.2). All 311 businesses said that their business had developed an explicit CX strategy/management/division plan. More than a third of the firms (37.3%) introduced the program two years ago, another third (33.8%) three to five years ago and the remainder (28.9%) over five years ago. All respondents were involved, either fully (33.4%) or partially (66.6%), in the development, implementation, and execution of these plans. The CX strategies and programs were developed mainly in the United States (30.5%), Canada (19.3%), Australia (19.3%), and the United Kingdom (19.9%).

TABLE 5.1   Respondents' and firms' demographics

Demographics	No of Respondents	Percentage of respondents	Demographics	No of Respondents	Percentage of respondents
Respondents' age			**Firm's headquarters**		
18–29 years	33	10.6	USA	100	32.2
29–45 years	143	46.0	UK	62	19.9
46 years or older	135	43.4	Australia	56	18.0
	311	100.00	Canada	55	17.7
			Other (Finland, Sweden, Norway	38	12.2
			Total	311	100.00
Respondents' length of employment with firm			**Respondents' firm's age**		
3–5 years	104	58.2	3–5 years	121	38.9
More than 5 years	207	41.8	1–2 years	34	10.9
Total	311	100.00	More than 5 years	156	50.2
			Total	311	100.0
Respondents' length of time in their current position			**Firm's offerings**		
Less than 5 years	8	2.6	Services	154	49.5
6–10 years	49	15.8	Goods	157	50.5
11–30 years	123	39.5	**Total**	311	100.00
More than 30 years	131	42.1			
Total	311	100.0			
Respondents' positions in their firm			**Business type**		
CEO	33	10.6	Business services	71	22.8

(continued)

TABLE 5.1 Continued

Demographics	No of Respondents	Percentage of respondents	Demographics	No of Respondents	Percentage of respondents
Executives/ directors (marketing/ sales/customer experience)	77	24.8	Consumer goods	73	23.5
Managers (business, account, customer experience, marketing, brand)	114	36.7	Business goods	84	27.0
Others	87	27.9	Consumer services	83	26.7
Total			Total	311	100
			Number of employees in respondents' firm		
			Less than 20	67	21.5
			21–100	47	15.1
			101–500 employees	60	19.3
			501–1000 employees	36	11.6
			More than 1000	101	32.5
			Total	311	100.0

The aim of our analysis was to identify and profile groups of firms with distinctly different attitudes and behaviors about CX management. The analysis, in its essence, confirmed our three CX management practices – those of Preservers, Transformers, and Vanguards. The cluster size, however, differed significantly. Vanguards represented 19 percent of all firms and Transformers approximately 45 percent, while the remaining 36 percent can be

TABLE 5.2 Firms' activities

Activities	Number of respondents	Percentage of respondents	Activities	Number of respondents	Percentage of respondents
Is a customer experience plan/ strategy developed			**Country customer experience plan developed**		
Yes	311	100.0	USA	95	30.5
No	0	0	Canada	60	19.3
Total	311	100.00	UK	62	20.0
			Australia	60	19.3
			Other (Finland and Sweden)	33	10.9
			Total	311	100.00
The CE program/ strategy was introduced			**Mean sales growth figure for past 3 years**		
Less than 1 year ago	24	7.7	Did not change/ decreased	58	18.6
1–2 years ago	92	29.6	Increased by 1%	141	45.4
3–5 years ago	105	33.8	Increased by 11%	80	25.7
More than 5 years ago	90	28.9	Increased by more than 21%	32	10.3
	311	100.0	**Total**	311	100.0
Involvement in CX Plan development					
Fully involved	181	33.4			
Partially involved	130	66.6			
Total	311	100.00			

considered Preservers. Next, we used the cluster analysis data to establish the crucial link between the different practices and the firms' performance. Guided by other well-cited and established key research (e.g., Coviello et al. 2002), we chose sales growth as the most valid measurement of firms' performance. As finance scholars advised us, sales growth is often a better indicator for profitability than declared profitability itself. The latter is often artificially reduced in order to keep resulting tax payments as low as possible. Next, we analyzed the performance of all 311 firms. The results were encouraging. Apparently, CX is good business – 63.0 percent of the firms we investigated in our global study achieved sales growth for the last three-year period. Moreover, 16 percent of the firms with an explicit CX management program reported growth levels of 11 percent or more.

Before we analyzed the performance by cluster, we investigated whether the firms of each cluster could have something in common, and if so, what. We used various demographic variables as covariates (to determine whether they had a significant influence), and they were included one at a time and then all together. Covariates included the age of the respondent, length of employment with the firm, position in the firm, length of time in their current position; also the age of the respondent's firm, its headquarters, offerings, business type, number of employees, whether they exported and sales growth. Unfortunately, no definite conclusions could be reached. Some of these factors were significant on their own, but when combined with others, they lost their significance. For example, the Vanguard cluster included firms' headquarters in all the countries of our sample; it was split between B2B and B2C orientation; it was spread from services to poor manufacturing, from young to established firms, from health care to the automotive industry; it had ranges of less than 100 to more than 10,000 employees. While this might be unfortunate from a statistical viewpoint, it provides us with a great insight. It is a message of hope and evidence: CX management practice is NEITHER context-specific, NOR dependent upon company size, industry sector, or location. The same rules apply for everyone.

CX management practice is NEITHER context-specific, NOR dependent upon company size, industry sector, or location

Now, the important question: Which CX strategy outperforms the others? And, by how much does it outperform the others?

Before we reveal our findings, let's play a little game, and see if you can guess the correct answer.

Reflecting on everything that we know so far about CX management practice, fill in your personal ranking of the three clusters, Preservers, Transformers, and Vanguards below – Number 1 being the best, Number 3 the worst-performing cluster, (by comparison, that is, because we have already established that there is a strong business case for a CX strategy). Think about the most compelling reason for why you believe Preservers, Transformers, or Vanguards perform best and add it next to your choice. The last column is simply for some "added fun." Try to guess how much better your Number 1 and Number 2 perform. Use Number 3 as your benchmark. For example, if you believe Preservers are your Number 1, Transformers are Number 2, and Vanguards are Number 3, give the worst performer a score of 100. Use this score to determine the value of Number 2. For example, if you believe Transformers outperform Vanguards by 20 percent, your Transformers score is 120, etc.

Ranking Cluster	Most compelling reason	Performance
1.		
2.		
3.		100

In the next chapter, we will reveal the numbers, so you can check how you did. Good luck!

6

Your CX Management Balance Sheet: Where Are You and Where Do You Want to Be? How to Get from A (Current State) to B – A Step-by-Step Approach

And the winner is …?

Ranking Cluster	Most compelling reason	Performance
1. Vanguards	Holistic strategy execution	600
2. Transformers	Being caught in the middle	250
3. Preservers	Measurement isn't important	100

In terms of annual average sales growth during the last three years, this converts into Vanguards 12 percent, Transformers 5 percent, Preservers 2 percent. In terms of performance, the lowest variance, as in performance values deviating from the average, is found in the Vanguard cluster, while the widest spread is, almost by definition, present in the Transformer cluster. Of course, there are slight differences inside the clusters, too. For example, not all Vanguards perform equally, but the overall message in terms of who is outperforming whom across all sectors, industries, and other possible factors, is clear – Vanguards.

Let's reflect on these findings and see how your estimates compare with the empirical data. Did you rank the groups in the correct order? If yes, what was the most compelling reason for your decision? How does your perception differ from reality, if at all? Did you correctly guess the scores, and, in particular, the significant differences in performance? Perhaps you thought that Preservers would be the best performers. Your argument could have been that their efforts are process driven, relying on what they know, not investing in something managers can't comprehend, and therefore following the cost-driven-value strategy. You might have thought that, by investing heavily in an almost change-management-like CX strategy effort, Vanguards can only outperform their competitors somewhere in the distant future. Or maybe you hypothesized that Transformers have the best of both worlds and will therefore outperform the others. These are all plausible arguments, but this book is not about discussing plausibility – instead, it offers evidence that can be translated into actionable results. So, let's start by talking about benchmarking. In order to benchmark, we first have to establish a "status quo."

First things first – what cluster do you belong to?

In order to determine how to design, implement, manage, and/or improve a firm's CX strategy, we have to establish their current practices. In the following, we focus on the typology's anchor points, the Vanguards and Preservers, and discuss their practices in detail. If your firm, or a firm you know, and/or one you investigate falls into neither of these categories, it is a Transformer.

Let's remind ourselves really quickly of the main differences between Preservers, Transformers, and Vanguards over all five CX management practice dimensions (see Table 4.1).

TABLE 4.1   Customer experience practice typology

	Typology		
	Preservers	**Transformers**	**Vanguards**
Definition, Scope and Objectives	Extension of service.	Acknowledge the broad nature of CE and its strategic importance.	Broad and strategic. No other priority "tops" it.
Governance	Functional level and initiatives. Focus within the firm.	Link CE to organizational goals and strategy.	Policy and operational levels aligned. Continual assessment and improvement.
Management (Operational)	Service quality, channel integration.	Focus on channel integration, customer loyalty, brand perception, and recommendations.	Integration of business processes through the supply chain and across channels. Commensurate HR and Organizational Development policies.
Policy Development	Lack of overarching vision.	Strategic intent, which varies as to sponsorship.	Committed top-level sponsorship, cross-functional ownership.
Challenges	Not a strategic initiative, cannot make the business case for change.	Looking for senior sponsorship, more appropriate metrics, business, and process models.	Reinvention, and maintaining competitive edge. Business partners sometimes a limiting factor.

Vanguards – The cream of the crop …

Now we will take a more in-depth look at Vanguards' CX practices. All Vanguards agree that the CX, its measurement, and subsequent established link to their firm's performance are important. These firms embark on a CX program as a means of addressing what they define as "emerging" customer demands. Vanguards perceive CX as an essential part of their brand. They believe that CX is the most common denominator for brand value reinforcement. Vanguards specify CX as a key strategic objective for the

entire firm, and its impact on business performance
is consistently managed and measured across all
functions and departments. Vanguards employ
CX (and equivalent) measures to evaluate
the impact of CX on performance. In
order to do this, they aim to quantify CX's impact on customer satisfaction, customer recommendations,
and business performance. Vanguards'
use of these measures is based upon their
confidence that their customers' expectations
are the key building block of their CX strategy and
practice. Therefore, customer touch-points, such as customer-facing people,
are viewed as the focal point of their CX program. Moreover, through the
certainty that CX is primarily associated with the quality of their service,
Vanguards emphasize that providing excellent customer experience creates
a strong emotional bond between the firm and their customers. Such firms
are able to identify many incidents where good or bad customer experience
impacted their business. Vanguards constantly work on improving existing
measurements of their CX delivery through a comprehensive discussion
and acknowledgment of the measurements' limitations. Not only are CX
measurements and outcomes important to Vanguards, but so too is CX
planning and management. The path to a successful strategy, however,
is often not as straightforward as initially thought. In some instances, CX
started as a pilot project and gradually gained momentum, often referred
to as an "evolutionary" change approach. In other instances, the CX strategy
was more "revolutionary," changing the way business is done, often literally
overnight. In both cases, CX has a major impact on strategy and the way
business is done. Vanguards display clear CX business models that define
(as precisely as possible) the CX concept, its purpose, expected outcomes,
and the resources it will receive. As part of their planning, Vanguards not
only develop CX strategies based upon all stakeholders' CX perceptions, but
use CX perceptions often as new paradigms of their firm's overall strategy,
and, subsequently, employee management. The CX strategy and resulting
objectives are developed through formal and transparent strategy and

planning processes. The planning efforts involve CX classification development, CX boundary settings, CX measurements, CX aims, and relating CX management efforts to specific financial outcomes.

It doesn't end here, though, and in the holistic, overarching CX philosophy, various other actions are taken to ensure the CX strategy's success. These actions include, but aren't limited to, the following: integrating functions and business units across the organization in the CX management process; integrating supply chain management as a vital CX strategy and management factor; assessing individual employees' contributions and amending their remuneration, rewards, and promotion structure upon their individual impact on the customer experience; frequent CX progress and best practice reporting (the latter is often used for CX training purposes). Vanguards, with respect to CX values, while not necessarily agreeing upon what they consider to be best service (definitions range from a service that the customer does not even recognize to doing something extra and unanticipated), put the customers viewpoint clearly in the center of all judgments about its effectiveness. Vanguards' CX strategy and program enjoy the strong and visible support of the most senior managers of the firm. Almost everyone in the organization knows who or what event started their CX program, and who or which group is responsible for managing CX, reporting on its outcomes and developing its practices. Vanguards also believe that delivering excellent customer experience might change by market, location, and other contextual factors.

Yet another differentiating set of Vanguards' CX practice characteristics revolves around their firms' CX values, as reflected in their employee management. Vanguards emphasize the central role their employees play in providing consistent CX across all touch-points. Predictably, Vanguards state that linking customer-facing employees with back office/operational systems is vital to delivering excellent customer experiences. Employees' contributions to CX form an important part of Vanguards' HR management training, recruitment, and rewards policies. In particular, customer-facing employees are trained in delivering excellent CX. This training often starts with awareness exercises about the firm's motivations and objectives for achieving superior customer experiences. Employees – sometimes referred to as "CX ambassadors" – are expected to act in accordance with the firm's brand and CX values during all dealings with customers and suppliers alike. Now we have gained a comprehensive understanding of Vanguards' CX strategies and management practices, we shift our attention to the second anchor point of the CX strategy and management policy typology – the Preservers.

The other side of the story – the Preservers

At the other extreme of the typology are the Preservers, which in most cases display the opposite of the Vanguards' CX management practices. For example, Preservers strongly disagree with the fact that CX measurement and its link to outcomes is important. For them, not only are CX-specific measures non-existent, but the business case for CX (e.g., relating it to other existing measures of service quality and customer satisfaction) is absent and, according to respondents' own statements, often "not desired." This is slightly startling, given the fact that all Preserver firms have developed what they describe as an explicit CX strategy and corresponding management structure. CX, while portrayed as strategy, displays no connection to brand, brand attachment, and brand values in Preservers' firms. Preservers' CX practice origins are often vaguely defined or unknown, and firms are unable to provide examples of either good or bad customer experience. One common driver appears to be the fact that CX addresses competitor pressure, rather than a change in consumer demands. There is little evidence that Preservers consider top-management support crucial for their program's success. This is not the only instance in which Preservers display a unidirectional view; a "we-know–what-is-best-for-our-customers" approach is omnipresent. Preservers' CX management programs are located in only one department – in most instances marketing – and they do not display the urge to expand their program in the firm's other functions and departments. There is no evidence that Preservers connect front- and back-office integration as a crucial part of CX management. Preservers do not deem that all channels are important in forming the customer experience perception. They posit that it is only critical incidents, often associated with service recovery, that will ultimately drive consumer/customer behaviour. Preservers, following this logic, do not, in the vast majority of instances, invest in their customer-facing personnel. There are no explicit training programs emerging from, or influenced by, their CX management program. Personnel are generally seen as a cost position, rather than an asset in delivering desirable customer experiences. Given the fact that Preservers' focus is on customer interactions based upon service recovery, the CX management program often emphasizes call-center management to handle most instances of customers contacting the firm with a problem they are encountering with the firm's offering. This displays a reactive, rather than proactive understanding of CX dynamics and their management. In this instance, Preservers believe that CX does not mean that they should attempt to manage these interactions so that the customer receives something extra and unexpected. It is interesting to note that while Preservers often use suppliers to manage what they consider crucial parts of the customer experience, they disagree with the view that suppliers and business partners are an integral part of their CX management program. It appears that CX in Preservers' companies is often seen as a "tick in the box" rather than a strategic initiative, and is often driven by cost-cutting opportunities, such as outsourcing customer service and call-centers, rather than (willingness to gain) an understanding of what the most profitable firms and researchers alike define as CX's true nature.

In-between these two polar opposite groups are Transformers, with varying degrees of emphasis of the different CX dimensions (see Chapter 4). Transformers consider the positive link between CX and financial performance, and acknowledge CX's holistic nature and the consequential tasks in scoping and outlining its management. They display an ongoing CX strategy and management practice discussion. Unlike Preservers, Transformers deem customer-facing personnel as vital in CX management. Transformers credit CX as a key influencer of their customers' satisfaction, loyalty, recommendations, and brand perception. Transformers judge CX as strategically important and underscore the inevitability of designing and achieving a matching strategy based upon their CX definition.

Transformers link CX practice to executive goals and current measures of customer outcomes. However, Transformers recognize the inadequacies of current measures and pursue more refined methodologies to evaluate CX and its impact on their firm's performance. Transformers express a comprehensive history of their programs. Transformers have visibly selected individuals as CX champions. These individuals do not necessarily establish a central and cross-departmental team. Transformers acknowledge the impact of customer-facing employees in providing CX, thereby inducing the desired customer behavior, and develop suitable instruction and coaching programs. Transformers try to become a CX-focused organization, admitting both the all-encompassing nature of CX and the consequences of managing CX throughout the firm. Their firms acknowledge long-term commitment as necessary for a successful conversion. Nonetheless, they struggle to develop a CX business model and the corresponding business processes, with the result that they end up focusing attention on managing existing systems rather than developing and embracing new ones. Transformers struggle to link CX to financial outcomes, but are convinced of the positive influence of CX on customer behavior and organizational goals.

During our comprehensive study we could detect that, as mentioned earlier, there were variances inside each cluster. For example, we saw that some of the Transformers' overall practices are not much more advanced than those of the Preservers, while others have almost reached Vanguard status. Moreover, practices inside the firm can often display different characteristics, depending on the individual strategic emphasis of different dimensions of the CX management program. By way of illustration, some of the Vanguards clearly emphasized the role of operational management, as in, for example, the importance of customer-facing personnel, making this a top priority; others, however, ranked governance efforts more highly, as indicated by their emphasis on measuring CX and linking it to the firm's profitability and other key performance indicators. In summary, the data clearly indicates that there is what could be considered a continuum of practices, ranging from Preservers to Vanguards.

Moving from status quo to desired state

You should now be able to allocate your firm, or the firm in question, to one of the three clusters of CX strategy and management practice: Preservers, Transformers, and Vanguards.

Next, we need to discuss whether it is both desirable and feasible for the firm in question to metamorphose from one CX strategy and management practice to another? While in some exceptional circumstances it might be feasible to move from what our research identified as more profitable practice, such as that of the Vanguards, towards a lower performance cluster, such as Transformers or Preservers, we will focus on what we believe to be the most logical step, that is, "moving up the ladder" to (ultimately) become a Vanguard.

In order to develop and execute more profitable CX strategies, a firm has to demonstrate the ability to develop dynamic capabilities. A dynamic capability refers to an asset beyond an accountant's balance-sheet-determined viewpoint, accentuating the hidden "soft" management assets to stimulate, and the successful arrangement of resources from both inside and outside the firm. Remember, for example, how Vanguards use both internal and external CX ambassadors to orchestrate the perfect CX delivery.

Think of dynamic capabilities as three constellations of activities: sensing, seizing, and transforming. To sense is to identify and assess an opportunity, such as the importance of CX as the next competitive battleground. To seize is to acquire and deploy all necessary resources to identify and capture value – for example, by purchasing this book. To transform is to continuously work and renew these opportunities – recall the Vanguards' practice of constantly searching for new ways to measure and manage the impact of their CX management practice. This indicates that Vanguards are aware that even despite (or because of) their current status, the constant search for improvement is a fundamental part of a successful CX DNA.

These three activities, sensing, seizing, and transforming, are, according to our findings, prerequisites if the firm is to build a sustainable, competitive CX strategy. Vanguards appear to have developed stronger dynamic CX capabilities than their competitors across all five dimensions of CX strategy and management practices. Our typology therefore allows firms a framework based upon our empirical research and the proven ability and impact of dynamic capabilities to develop the most successful CX strategies and management practices.

Vanguards appear to have developed stronger dynamic CX capabilities than their competitors across all five dimensions of CX strategy and management practices

By reading these lines, you have already demonstrated your sensing capabilities. Seizing capabilities include designing a CX strategy and business models to deliver the experiences your customers desire and to capture value for the firm at the same time, just as Vanguards do. In order to succeed, the CX strategy needs to include secure access to both capital and human resources. Employees and their CX delivery and management skills are vital. Good incentive design, based upon the customers' perceptions of their experience is a compulsory but not sufficient condition for superior performance in this area. Vanguards prove that strong relationships must also be forged externally with suppliers, fulfillers, and customers alike.

The toughest part – transforming

The need for transforming capabilities is most obvious when radical new opportunities are to be addressed, such as developing a successful CX strategy and management practice. A word of warning, though: please objectively evaluate the strengths and weaknesses of the company before venturing into unknown territory. If you need assistance in this matter, please see our offer of free evaluation of your firm and support at the end of this chapter.

The key three

I thought long and hard, speaking with colleagues, managers, thought-leaders, researchers, and consultants, about how best to assist you and your efforts in the transformation process. In the end, it all comes back to establishing superior performance as the key component of the firm's CX activities. As a result, I returned to scrutinizing the results of our global study to determine which individual factors are the key drivers of Vanguards' profitability. In order to stay true to the spirit of *Measuring Customer Experience* in transferring insight into actions, I focus on the three key drivers of CX strategy and management practices. Please be aware that ALL factors are important in successfully transforming your firm towards the most profitable practices. However, based on our everyday experience with clients and firms, it is best to focus first on a few CX key drivers that have an immediate and measurable impact on performance. Building evidence and accountability is, after all, known as one of the central components in driving successful strategic transformation. All three key drivers are equally important in driving performance, so, rather than numbering them, we used letters to identify them as follows:

A. Measuring CX
B. CX from the customers' viewpoint
C. CX delivery – the crucial role of employees

From a performance perspective, understanding the impact of varying degrees of CX planning and management, measurement, values, and other issues on profitability is important. The understanding gained from the three key CX management practices will assist firms in building a successful CX strategy. We now take a look at them one by one, guiding you through how to evolve from your current status in relation to each of the three towards becoming a Vanguard.

Measuring CX

Measuring customer experience is on the mind of every CX manager, no matter whether the firm is a Preserver, Transformer, or Vanguard. However, there are different opinions about its importance. While

Preservers believe it is not a main concern, and trust their established measurement approaches (e.g., customer satisfaction), Transformers recognize that CX requires more than just adding one question to existing measurements in order to truly evaluate the CX and its impact on outcomes, such as loyalty and word-of-mouth. However, they struggle with how and where to measure customer experience in a comprehensive way. Most Transformers use a measurement they believe can at least measure a possible outcome of a good experience, such as the customers' willingness to recommend their offerings, as measured by the NPS. Vanguards, unlike others, have a more sophisticated approach to measuring CX, and in Chapters 7 and 8 I will discuss the challenge of successfully measuring, and therefore managing CX, including detailed examples of how firms have transformed into Vanguards using EXQ (a measurement of customer experience quality). Unlike Preservers and Transformers, Vanguards aim for a systematic analysis of customers' expectations, the experience delivered at all points of customer contact and the effectiveness of the processes they deploy to deliver CX. This signifies an entirely different approach, going beyond acknowledgment, sensing, and then entering the stage of seizing. Vanguards acknowledge that traditional measurements, such as customer satisfaction, service quality, and the likelihood of recommendation have certain shortcomings, in particular in the context of CX. These measurements often measure only an intention, not true consumer behavior. It is a well-established fact in research that intentions differ, often significantly, from behavior. Setting aside the evidence from research, let's take an example "closer to home." Are you familiar with the tradition of New Year's resolutions? At the stroke of midnight on December 31st, people in most Western countries celebrate the beginning of the New Year and make a commitment to doing something that will makes a positive difference, such as spending more time with the family, losing weight, etc. Now recall your resolutions over the last three years – how many of them translated into (measurable and established) outcomes and changes? Can you detect a discrepancy between intention and behavior? If yes, I believe you understand the point I am trying to make. Vanguards, unlike others, such as word-of-mouth behavior, purchasing behavior, repurchasing behavior, share-of-category, and share-of-wallet. The second main difference is that Vanguards understand that measuring an outcome alone, which is "what" and "how" customers are doing, is not comprehensive enough to understand the customer experience. Instead, Vanguards focus in an exploratory way on why customers do what they do. Only combined with the "why," do the "what" and "how" truly make sense, thereby allowing Vanguards to investigate and manage CX in the best possible way. This also requires new thinking in terms of which methods are being used to gain insight, such as observatory techniques (e.g., ethnography and nethnography) and other qualitative methods. The common denominator of all these techniques and the Vanguards' approach is that they start with a blank sheet regarding what constitutes CX, seeing it from the customers' viewpoint. In order to gain true insight, no preconceptions are allowed. In summary, in order to move from your current CX practices towards the most profitable ones, you need to follow these steps:

1. Measure behavior, not intentions.
2. Use existing measures, such as customer satisfaction and NPS, as complementary measurements, and do not just focus on your insight.
3. Gain insight by losing your perceptions about what you believe customers experience. Remember that 80 percent versus 8 percent example. Be open-minded.
4. Explore rather than confirm what constitutes the customer experience.
5. Talk with, not to, your customers to gain true insights.
6. Use this exploratory, qualitative insight to develop your own measurement, or use measurements that are developed to measure behavior based upon the holistic CX, such as EXQ.

Customer experience from the customers' viewpoint

Measuring CX and, in particular, the points outlined for developing a successful CX measurement go hand-in-hand with exploring the customer experience from the customer's viewpoint. Vanguards execute this part of CX management almost flawlessly by incorporating the knowledge and insight gained from measuring CX throughout all possible CX influencers. The term "CX influencers" refers to all of the customers' direct and indirect interactions with the firm and their offerings. It does sound rather simple when you listen to Vanguards – all one has to do is listen attentively to your customers. However, this often requires more than just listening skills. As a matter of fact, it requires a different mindset, a different CX philosophy. I am often asked what the main difference is between Vanguards' and all other CX strategies and management practices, and I believe I can summarize it in one statement: Vanguards are not competing against (other firms), they are competing FOR (their customers). All CX insights, efforts, and practices revolve around delivering the best possible experience from a customer's viewpoint. All of the Vanguards' practices, not just the customer-facing ones, are based upon what the customer experiences. Gaining insight about how customers perceive their experiences is a cornerstone of their CX strategy, and all functions and departments collect and freely share insights in an open, all-access platform model. Best practice and all experiences are shared freely not only across the entire firm but also with all suppliers, business partners, and customers alike. Social media plays a key role in gaining this insight and engaging all stakeholders. Personnel are hired on the skills that enhance the customer experience in their context. Often these are considered "soft" skills, such as the ability to listen, comfort, and display empathy towards a customer. Another example is the fact that Vanguards' employees' bonuses and career progression are not based upon sales numbers, but upon how their customers perceived their experiences, leading to the next point, CX delivery. The step-by-step approach to moving towards becoming an insightful CX Vanguard is as follows:

1. Change the way the firm views the customer. Everything revolves around the CX, and everyone contributes.
2. Ask your customers about how they experience all their interactions with your firm, prior, during, and after the purchase of your offerings. CX doesn't end with a sale; it often just begins with it.
3. Compete for your customer, not against others.
4. Listen to your customers, and observe and engage with them. Take note, and, most importantly, tell them what you did to address their concerns, challenges, and suggestions – always give feedback to feedback.

5. Share your insights, examples, and best practice across the entire firm; CX needs to become embedded in your firm's DNA.
6. Adopt an outside-in versus inside-out CX approach.

CX delivery – the crucial role of employees

Vanguards, unlike their peers, integrate all of the firm's activities across all channels to provide a consistently good experience as defined by the customer. We established that, unlike TQM and service quality approaches, which aim to cut the customer experience into small manageable episodes, Vanguards focus on customer assessment of an overall experience as a summary of all direct and indirect interactions. Vanguards know that customer-facing employees are a key component of how their customers build their CX assessment. Thus, they do everything in their power to ensure the right people with the right tools are in the right place at the right time – that is, where the customer, not the firm, perceives they will be. Technology is seen as a great enabler, evident in the aim of integrating front-office and back-office operations to provide the information needed in order for customer-facing employees to deliver the experiences their customers desire. But, what is more important for Vanguards is that their employees should have both the right skills (i.e., an ideal match according to the customer's perception of their experience at any particular point and time) and the freedom to act independently according to the current situation. Vanguards believe that this autonomy reflects their trust, and trusted employees feel valued and satisfied. Vanguards invest heavily in employee training, basing this on the belief that happy employees deliver great customer experiences. Far-reaching communication programs encourage customer-facing employees to become self-reflective experts, thus improving their ability to provide the experiences their customers desire. Vanguards know that CX requires more from employees than simply following uniform processes and rules, more than service with a smile, so to speak. CX is still, even for Vanguards, challenging to define, and employees are required to think past "mission accomplished" and encourage the CX's emotional aspect. It's not an easy task, but Vanguards are constantly developing and amending their practices to address this challenge. A step-by-step approach towards developing a Vanguard customer-facing practice among employees is outlined below:

1. Acknowledge the importance of customer-facing employees in forming the customer experience.
2. Hire the "right" people according to the experiences your customers are looking for – think "soft" versus "hard" skills, and vice versa.
3. Use technology as an enabler to give employees access to all the information they require to deliver the experience the customer is looking for.
4. Invest in your employees – it will pay off.
5. Demonstrate trust by giving employees the autonomy and authority to act upon the CX needs.
6. Go beyond the "service with a smile" attitude.

You now have a great starting point from which you can depart on your journey to become a Vanguard. We offered three different options to establish a successful CX strategy, based upon the three key drivers of profitability. In the next chapter we will take an in-depth look at how you can use one of these key factors, measuring customer experience, to embark on the successful mission of developing and executing the most profitable CX strategies.

A unique offer ...

Measuring Customer Experience is about giving you as much support as you can possibly require. If you are still in doubt about where you sit on the typology (i.e., is my firm, or the firm I are working with, a Preserver, Transformer, or Vanguard?), I offer you a unique opportunity: follow the link http://tinyurl.com/Measure-CX-Evaluation, answer a few questions to assist us in our research, and we will conduct a FREE analysis of your CX strategy and management practices, detailing not only your cluster and your ranking, but also delivering a suggested list of actions in order of highest impact on firm performance, based upon our extensive global studies.

chapter 7

The Devil Is in the Details – Only What Get Measured Gets Managed

Management guru Peter Drucker once said, "[only] what gets measured, gets managed." As we could clearly document, this applies in particular to the challenges firms face in measuring their customers' experience and its impact on the firm's performance. Even Vanguards see the measurement of CX as a, if not the, key challenge for their CX strategy's success.

> If done appropriately, as is evident in the data presented in Chapter 6, measuring CX is the key driver for success and profitability.

Before we dive into possible measurements, we need to reflect upon what we already know about measures that are currently used to evaluate the customer experience and its influence on customer behavior. The best departure point for this exploration is investigating why and how these measures originated.

Business and marketing practices have evolved from bringing goods "to market," through a stage of market and consumer targeting ("marketing to"), towards the latest focus on a "market with customers/suppliers/employees/stakeholders." The latter is often expressed as a shift to co-creating value with customers over an extended time frame. Co-creation connects the firm's network of relationships with customers' capabilities, enabling customers to achieve higher-order goals or objectives. These higher-order goals are coined "value-in-use." Value-in-use, in simple terms, states that the majority of customers' value perceptions of products and services arise during their use, not prior to or during the purchase phase. Other researchers describe a similar development of practices from transaction to building relationships and ultimately networks wherein the firm's capabilities and assets facilitate customers creating value directly with other participants in a networked environment. This resembles some of the Vanguards' strategies we discussed earlier. While each of these perspectives regarding the evolution has its own conceptualization and terminology, they all present, to a great extent, equivalent and complementary views on the changing focus of practice and how customers perceive the value of a firm's offerings.

This rapid evolution of "paradigms" mirrors our contemporary marketplace, in which competition is moving from products to services and then to a post-product, post-service phenomenon that is still evolving and not yet fully formed. This is the new competitive battleground – *"Customer Experience"* (e.g., Klaus and Maklan 2007).

The term *"experience economy"* possibly originates with Pine and Gilmore (Gilmore & Pine II 1997; Gilmore & Pine II 2002), who make the obvious claim that experience represents a move beyond products and service. Their work, echoed by many at that time, focused the discussion of experience upon highly experiential environments such as American Girl dolls (2004), Harley Davidson outings (Schouten & McAlexander 1995) or white water rafting (Arnould & Price 1993). Nonetheless, their work helped researchers and firms alike to "rediscover" that people buy goods and services as a means of fulfilling deeper emotional, sensory, and even hedonic desires.

Experience management goes beyond the extraordinary; it is the mundane and everyday experience that drives behavior.

If we see the customer's world through this lens, we realize it is about how they experience the entire process of searching, acquiring, integrating, and deploying in order to achieve their aspirations (i.e. what matters most to them). However, there is no clear consensus about how firms can measure these customer experiences. Based upon our comprehensive studies conducted over the last eight years, we can confidently state that most firms committed to focusing on a product- and/or service-oriented quality, rather than CX quality. These limited views on how customers perceive their experience does not help firms to assess how customers evaluate their offerings.

Service quality vs. CX

Service quality is the gap between customers' expectations and their overall assessment (perceptions) of the service encounter (Parasuraman et al. 1988). This popular concept of the gap led to the widespread management motto of needing to "delight" customers by always exceeding their expectations. By far the most popular measure of service quality is SERVQUAL, and its commercial equivalent "Rater," a 22-item scale whose dimensions are reliability, assurance, tangibility, empathy, and responsiveness. Firms using Rater focus on a particular service episode and ask customers to assess the dimensions against their prior expectations using a 5-point Likert scale (Morrison Coulthard 2004).

SERVQUAL/Rater has been challenged conceptually, methodologically, and with respect to the validity of its dimensions. Rather than discussing the challenges that make these measures unsuitable for firms' CX focus, I will use the discussion to visualize what an appropriate measure of experience quality should look like.

(1) Researchers contest the notion that customers evaluate service or experience against their expectations (Cronin Jr. & Taylor 1992). Rater's generalizibility is questionable due to the fact that research has failed to validate its dimensions (Buttle 1996). Experience exposes a customers' overall assessment of value rather than in relation to expectations. It lacks

the attributes reflecting customers' higher-order objectives that lead to purchasing behavior.

(2) SERVQUAL focuses largely upon customers' assessments of the service process and human interactions (Mangold & Babakus 1991; Cronin Jr. & Taylor 1992; Richard & Allaway 1993). Customer experience focuses on value-in-use. Individual components of an interaction with the firm may be assessed as "good quality," but that does not automatically mean that the overall experience is judged to be of high quality, nor does measuring the components of service quality ensure that customers achieve their desired outcomes. SERVQUAL reflects the quality management origins of service quality, a manufacturing-like breakdown into tiny pieces of complex service systems and the ensuing optimization of each component. This, however, does not correspond with how customers assess their overall experiences.

(3) SERVQUAL's dimensions are too limited (Sureshchandar et al. 2002) to fully capture customer experience. Researchers suggest a broader and holistic conceptualization, and therefore measure, of experience (Verhoef et al. 2009). Gentile et al. (2007, p. 397) suggest: "Customer experience [...] is strictly personal and implies the customer's involvement at different levels (rational, emotional, sensorial, physical, and spiritual)." These holistic definitions, while consistent with experience, are too broad to create a practical CX measurement. Most experience research focuses on highly experiential contexts, highlighting the extraordinary experience aspect (Sharma & Patterson 2000; Chandon et al. 2005). This naturally fascinating approach to experience makes it challenging to create a universal CX measure similar to SERVQUAL, customer satisfaction, or NPS.

(4) Customers take a longitudinal perspective when assessing their experiences and believe they have had experience with your firm even before they have bought something. These pre-purchase or pre-direct encounter experiences develop from advertising, promotion, and word-of-mouth.

Therefore, we need to measure customer experience before and after the service encounter(s) and account for both direct and indirect contacts and the ever-so-present peer influences (Berry et al. 2002; Payne et al. 2008).

This generates practical challenges for firms. Longer timeframes make it harder to distinguish experience from the overall brand perception. Too short a time perspective, and the firm risks assessing experience in an all-too-narrow fashion.

(5) Experience is likely to occur across channels – the cumulative effect of numerous encounters – rather than being driven by a single episode. We do not understand how consumers synthesize these multi-channel encounters into an overall assessment of experience, but it is likely not to be a pure addition of individual service episodes (Sharma & Patterson 2000; Chandon et al. 2005).

Experience is likely to occur across channels – the cumulative effect of numerous encounters – rather than being driven by a single episode

(6) Experience research should enable us to validate its effects upon customer behavior to improve accountability. Even strong advocates of the intuitive relationship cycle between service quality, customer satisfaction and customer behavior, admit that this chain is difficult to make both operational (Sureshchandar et al. 2002) and researchable (Zeithaml et al. 1996). Service quality suggests a positive link between quality and satisfaction. Experience measures, however, should be linked directly to "hard" customer behavior affecting profitability, such as repurchase.

In summary, continuing to measure service quality is likely to be necessary for most firms, but is not sufficient on its own. Researchers need to develop an appropriate measure for the concept of CX that conforms to the following rules:

1. It is based upon an overall cognitive and emotional assessment of value from the customers' point-of-view rather than evaluated against benchmarks or expectations.
2. It captures the value-in-use of the organization's offerings, not just the attributes of product and service delivery.
3. It assesses, as much as possible, emotional responses as well as the functional delivery of the organization's promise;
4. It determines a reasonable focal time period, sufficiently before and after the service delivery, to allow the customer to assess the experience over time and across channels.
5. It is validated against behavioral measures as well as attitudinal ones.

Based upon these findings, I decided, with the invaluable assistance of my colleagues, to embark on the journey of developing a generalizable CX measurement. This is how I did it.

The stage is set – measuring CX

I developed a measure for EXQ (customer experience quality) to identify not only what constitutes the customer experience, but also to explain important customer behavior, such as repurchasing, word-of-mouth recommendation (Samson 2006), share-of-category, and satisfaction (see Figure 7.1).

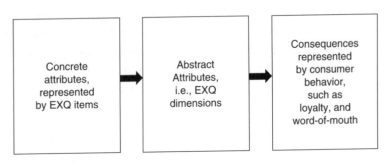

FIG 7.1 / **Explaining customer behavior**

I developed EXQ in four stages: (1) scale generation; (2) initial purification; (3) refinement; and (4) validation against the most important marketing outcomes. The stages are described briefly below (see Figure 7.2).

The focus of this book is not to deliver details about scale development methods; rather this is presented as an example to market researchers of how they might address the challenge of moving to a measure of customer experience.

Stage 1 – Scale generation explores what customers perceive their experience constitutes, based upon comprehensive qualitative studies. The analysis results in a preliminary scale containing items that represent five dimensions.

Stage 2 – Initial purification assesses the scale, using a representative sample of customers, of the context/firm/offering in question. Using Exploratory Factor Analysis (EFA), the scale is purified to the items that represent four customer experience dimensions.

Stage 3 – Refinement via Confirmatory Factor Analysis (CFA) validates the purified scale based on a representative sample and confirms the EXQ scale's reliability and validity.

Stage 4 – Validation is achieved by assessing the extent to which customer experience and its dimensions explain consumers' behavior.

Stage 1: scale generation

Stage 1 explores the perceptual attributes of experience through in-depth interviews using soft laddering (Grunert & Grunert 1995), a technique where respondents are restricted as little as possible in their natural flow of speech. This is an accepted method for assessing consumers' cognitive structures and underlying purchasing (Reynolds & Gutman 1988).

We achieved data saturation (Glaser & Strauss 1967) after conducting individual in-depth interviews with a sufficient number of customers according to the study's context. We used a random sample of existing, former, and potential customers that could comment on their individual experiences with the firm/context/offering in question.

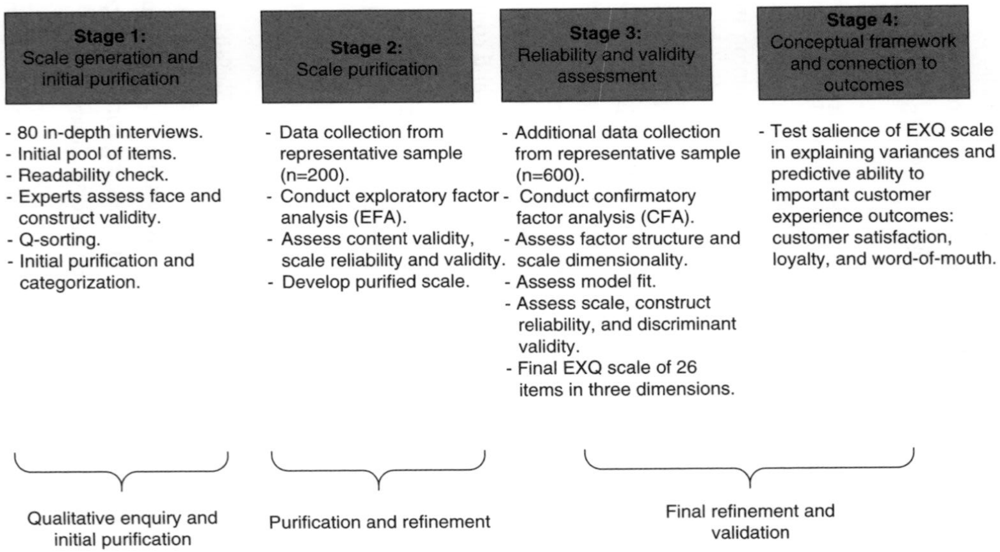

Stage 1:
Scale generation and
initial purification

- 80 in-depth interviews.
- Initial pool of items.
- Readability check.
- Experts assess face and
  construct validity.
- Q-sorting.
- Initial purification and
  categorization.

Qualitative enquiry and
initial purification

Stage 2:
Scale purification

- Data collection from
  representative sample
  (n=200).
- Conduct exploratory factor
  analysis (EFA).
- Assess content validity,
  scale reliability and validity.
- Develop purified scale.

Purification and refinement

Stage 3:
Reliability and validity
assessment

- Additional data collection
  from representative sample
  (n=600).
- Conduct confirmatory
  factor analysis (CFA).
- Assess factor structure and
  scale dimensionality.
- Assess model fit.
- Assess scale, construct
  reliability, and discriminant
  validity.
- Final EXQ scale of 26
  items in three dimensions.

Final refinement and
validation

Stage 4:
Conceptual framework
and connection to
outcomes

- Test salience of EXQ scale
  in explaining variances and
  predictive ability to
  important customer
  experience outcomes:
  customer satisfaction,
  loyalty, and word-of-mouth.

FIG 7.2 EXQ development process

The interviews were transcribed, coded, and analyzed following a grounded approach (Strauss & Corbin 1998). To maximize the content and face validity of the items generated, a panel of expert judges reviewed the retained item pool (Dagger et al. 2007) and performed three tasks: (1) they assessed the similarity of items, the clarity of phrasing and the terminology used in the scale; (2) they rated each item with respect to its relevance to the item description; and (3) they suggested dimensions and sub-dimensions that evolved from the research model and items. Five dimensions representing customer experience items resulted from this stage.

Stage 2: scale purification through EFA

The scale was purified through EFA. Data were collected through an online questionnaire accessible through a link sent to a sample of customers capable of assessing their experiences according to the context in question and meeting our strong data requirements.

EFA summarized the data into a minimum number of factors for prediction purposes. The resulting purified scale comprised three primary CX dimensions.

Stages 3 and 4: reliability and validity assessment through CFA

To perform the analysis, we collected a statistically relevant number of qualified responses through an online questionnaire accessible through a link to random customer samples according to our specifications. The exploratory and confirmatory analysis samples were analogous; they did not differ significantly in terms of demographics and represented the customer profile of the firm/context/offering in question. We measured the impact of customer experience on (re)purchasing behavior, word-of-mouth behavior (giving positive recommendations), share-of-category, and customer satisfaction.

My aim is to develop a CX quality scale that can be readily adapted to all types of firms. In order to develop a CX quality scale capable of serving this purpose, I adapted and extended the reliable and validated Silvestro, Fitzgerald, Johnston, and Voss (1992) service classification scheme (e.g., Auzair and Langfield-Smith 2005). Subsequently, I chose one professional service (wealth management: Hussain and Chong 2008), one mass service (fuel and service station: Jones 2008), and one service shop (retail banking: Silvestro 1999). In addition, I included a service reflecting the hedonic nature of CXs (lifestyle luxury goods retail) to ensure further cross-validation (Cronin et al. 2000). The CX scenarios I explored therefore varied in the degree to which the offering could be characterized as hedonic (lifestyle luxury goods) versus utilitarian (fuel and service station). Based upon these studies, EXQ was further verified across other industries, contexts, firms, and countries, and all studies confirmed EXQ's validity.

I am happy to share further data and information regarding method, questionnaire, results, and attendant validity testing with any interested readers.

EXQ – measuring customer experience

EXQ measures the customers' assessment of their experience quality on three dimensions representing 26 items: brand experience, service (firm) experience, and post-purchase/consumption experience (see Table 7.1).

Brand experience includes the customers' brand perceptions that influence their customer experience (Fitzsimons et al. 2008) and their

TABLE 7.1   EXQ scale

Customer experience quality scale EXQ		
Brand experience	*Service (provider) experience*	*Post-purchase/ consumption experience*
BRE1 Brand importance BRE2 Expertise – peace of mind BRE3 Independent advice BRE4 True costs BRE5 Importance service personal for brand BRE6 Value perception product BRE7 Value perception competitors	SPE1 Holding their hands SPE2 Process ease SPE3 Transparency SPE4 Flexibility SPE5 Multi-channel SPE6 Common grounding SPE7 Interpersonal skills SPE8 Importance of customer service SPE9 Personal relationship(s) SPE10 Servicescape SPE11 Efficient design	PPE1 Convenience retention PPE2 Familiarity PPE3 Proactively PPE4 Relationship versus transaction PPE5 Service recovery PPE6 Emotional reward PPE7 Social approval

decision process. Brand experience reflects customers' value perception of products, pricing, the "experience-delivering" personnel, the brand and of competitors' offerings in the search process of evaluating the firm's offerings (e.g., Hoch 2002). It includes components of the customers' social environment, such as their reference groups, peers, and other sources of information (e.g., social media and reviews) (e.g., Luo 2005). This is the part of the CX prior to purchase/acquisition.

Service (firm) experience embodies three themes associated with the experiences customers have when they interact with a firm's physical presence, personnel, policies, and practices. The first theme relates to the process experience, including items such as process ease and the challenge of using multiple channels in dealing with the provider (Lemke et al. 2011). The second theme relates to direct evaluations of encounters with personnel, such as common grounding or the existence of personal relationships with the personnel (Grace and O'Cass 2004). The third theme describes the influence of the physical environment, such as Servicescape (Bitner 1992). The fourth theme relates to what researchers consider situational and consumer moderators, such as task orientation and location (e.g., Dabholkar & Bagozzi 2002).

Post-purchase/consumption experience describes the customers' experiences encountered post-purchase and consumption of the offering in question (Payne et al. 2008). This dimension focuses on all post-purchase consumption, not just product-in-use. It covers perceptions of familiarity (Söderlund 2002), retention (Verhoef 2003), and service recovery (Kelley & Davis 1994), displaying signs of customer commitment to the service provider (Bansal et al. 2004). The dimension also includes expressions of emotions associated with social and hedonic value, referring to post-purchase pleasure and an increase in social status based on the relationship with the service provider (e.g., Sweeney & Soutar 2001).

Next, I focused on the important link between CX and customer behavior. Using EXQ, I measured the CX influence on repurchasing behavior, word-of-mouth behavior, share-of-category, and customer satisfaction. In order to further demonstrate the explanatory power of EXQ, I compared it with the predominant measure of service quality, SERVQUAL. This was achieved by collecting data from survey respondents answering in alternating format, first the EXQ, and normally 1–2 days later the SERVQUAL questionnaire (or vice versa).

EXQ demonstrated substantial and positive relationships between CX and both customer behavior and customer satisfaction. Looking at these relationships in more detail, we observe that brand experience has a great effect on customer satisfaction and word-of-mouth behavior. Brand experience also displays a great effect on repurchases. The service (firm) experience has the greatest effect of all three dimensions on customer satisfaction, a great effect on word-of-mouth behavior, and a high, but slightly lower, influence on repurchasing behavior.

> Post-purchase/consumption experience displays by far the greatest effect of all dimensions on repurchase and word-of-mouth behavior and a great effect on customer satisfaction.

Service quality, measured by SERVQUAL, was found to influence customer satisfaction and behavior. Based on the belief that CX is a new and improved conceptualization and measurement to explain and predict how customers behave, I tested whether CX, measured by EXQ, would have a greater total effect on customer behavior. When comparing the influence of both constructs on important marketing outcomes, CX was found to have a greater total effect on repurchases, and a significant higher positive impact on customer satisfaction and word-of-mouth behavior than service quality (see Table 7.2).

TABLE 7.2 EXQ vs. SERVQUAL – explaining and predicting behavior

	Customer Satisfaction	Loyalty	Word-of-Mouth
EXQ	86%	87%	88%
SERVQUAL	64%	58%	51%

Based upon these findings, I wanted to go a step further and explore how EXQ compares with another measurement that is often used – customer satisfaction – in terms of explaining and predicting customer behavior. I compared, using the same approach and rigor as in my previous studies, the influence of CX (using EXQ) and customer satisfaction on customer behavior. EXQ, in comparison with customer satisfaction, demonstrates stronger relationships between CX and loyalty than between customer satisfaction and loyalty. Compared with the relationship between customer satisfaction and word-of-mouth, I also established a more direct link between CX and word-of-mouth. Customer satisfaction is often put forward as a mediator between service quality and loyalty and word-of-mouth (Seiders et al. 2005), but this relationship has always been challenged, suggesting there might be constructs (e.g., CX) capable of predicting consumer behavior better than customer satisfaction (e.g., Koenig-Lewis & Palmer 2008). The results of our studies imply that

customer experience, measured by EXQ, is an even better predictor of both loyalty and word-of-mouth behavior.

Therefore, measures of customer experience (e.g., EXQ) should at least be considered alongside the more traditional means of assessing strategy – customer satisfaction and NPS – since CX measures, according to our research, are better and more direct predictors of consumer behavior (see Table 7.3).

In today's business environment and the age of the digital customer, firms need to put particular emphasis on word-of-mouth behavior. Word-of-mouth is considered a more and more important consumer behavior for several reasons. For example, word-of-mouth communication

TABLE 7.3   **EXQ vs. customer satisfaction – explaining behavior**

	Loyalty	Word of Mouth	Share of Category
EXQ	0.87	0.88	0.92
Customer satisfaction	0.65	0.81	0.59

provides face-to-face, often explicit, information that is highly credible (Brown et al. 2005). This information can influence others' beliefs about a firm and their offerings, subsequently altering consumers' intentions to purchase from the company the offering in question (Lutz 1975; Sheth & Parvatiyar 1995). Researchers offer satisfaction, and dissatisfaction, as word-of-mouth precursors. We established the significant positive impact of customer experience on word-of-mouth, and a stronger relationship than that achieved through customer satisfaction. The findings indicate customer experience to be not only one of the possible precursors but also the most significant driver of word-of-mouth (see Table 7.3).

What does this mean for your firm ...?

Through multiple studies, I developed and validated the three-dimensional EXQ scale. We established EXQ's superior explanatory and predictive powers by linking it to customer behavior, and comparing it with the well-established SERVQUAL and customer satisfaction measurements.

Firms, managers, and consultants can use EXQ as an analytical tool to detect poor and/or excellent CE performances across several functions within the firm and/or across various locations within the firm across time. Another application of EXQ is to benchmark your CX strategy and management program within the firm or a specific industry.

Customers base their CX quality assessment on three dimensions: *brand experience, service (firm) experience and post-purchase/consumption experience*. EXQ will improve your understanding of how customers evaluate CX quality by linking their evaluation to important marketing outcomes, namely customer satisfaction, loyalty, repurchasing, share-of-category, and word-of-mouth behavior.

All three CX dimensions have a positive and significant impact on your customers' behavior. This validates the notion that the

CX evaluation goes beyond the direct (service) encounter.

Customers assess the quality of their experience upon all direct and indirect encounters with every function of the firms, channels and touch-points, such as marketing communications, advertising, Internet presence and after-sales care (e.g., Payne et al. 2008; Voss et al. 2008). Once we move our investigation to an even more in-depth level, digging deeper into the CX, so to speak, we reveal the influence of each individual CX dimension on customer behavior. For example, brand experience – the pre-encounter dimension – has an equally significant influence on all forms of customer behavior. The service (firm) experience has the most significant influence of all dimensions on customer satisfaction, confirming the suggested causal chain between the service encounter and customer satis-faction (e.g., Parasuraman et al. 1988). However, the dimension of post-purchase/consumption has the greatest influence on loyalty, repurchase, and word-of-mouth behavior. Based on their own first-hand experiences with the firm, customers have the power to evaluate not only the firm's offerings, but also the experiences connected with these interactions. This highlights the importance of past experiences with the firm in developing positive behavioral intentions (Voss & Zomerdijk 2007) and influencing loyalty (e.g., Buttle & Burton 2002).

Our research establishes a clear link between CX quality, as measured by EXQ, customer behavior, and, ultimately, profitability. EXQ's three dimen-sions represent a timeline of how customers assess their experience and behave. First, brand experience describes the influence of all direct and indirect CXs prior to purchase, such as searching and pre-purchase evalua-tion. Next, the service (firm) experience describes customers' experiences of all direct interactions with the provider during the purchasing and selection process. The ensuing post-purchase/consumption experience describes the evaluation and possible outcomes of a customer's experi-ence with the firm after the purchase or the consumption/use of the offering. This is similar to the well-established notion of the customer journey, which is described as the customer's sequence of touch-points with the company in buying and obtaining service (Voss et al. 2008). The sequential three-dimensionality of CX quality highlights to firms that CX needs to be managed differently. EXQ demonstrates that firms need to be concerned not only with the purchase (service) encounter, but also with the experience prior to and after purchase and/or consumption (Dick & Basu 1994). In order to deliver this, confirming our typology and its link to profitability, successful CX management requires the integration of all the firm's touch-points, the processes influencing the CX, and the subsequent desired customer behavior, throughout the customer journey.

EXQ also tackles one of the main challenges in establishing a successful CX strategy – defining and clearly scoping the parts of CX that are influencing customer behavior.

Our studies provide empirical validation to the suggestions that CX goes beyond the evaluation of service quality or employee performance (e.g., Brocato et al. 2012), and the notion that the customer experience is a broader evaluation of the customers' interactions with the company (e.g., Verhoef et al. 2009). By connecting CX evaluations to behavior,

> EXQ eliminates all "the noise," and focuses purely on what drives behavior, and, as a result, profitability.

We can confidently state that

> CX isn't *everything*, and can be both, measured and managed.

Even if customers in interviews state all kinds of reasons regarding which part of their experience could have influenced their behavior, EXQ, by connecting CX to behavior and forcing the customer to rank the parts of their experiences according to importance, leads them to their actual decision and ranks the most important drivers. This allows a firm, just as our typology did, not only to prioritize their efforts, but also to develop a clear link to their key performance indicators and the firm's profitability.

Some people might challenge our research and point towards the absence of certain factors they believe should either influence the customer's experience assessment, or form part of a CX management program. Please allow me to remind you that *Measuring Customer Experience* is not about proving whether opinions and suggestions are right or wrong. The book develops rigorous, unbiased evidence for how a firm can develop the most profitable CX strategy, and how to measure the customer experience. Our research reports empirical evidence and offers explanations for why this evidence is found in order to allow you to "glimpse inside the machine," to improve your understanding of how CX works. We found no evidence supporting the claim that promotions and loyalty programs are part of the customers' experience perceptions. We can support the notion that pricing in terms of delivering what a customer views as good value is an important part of the customer experience (e.g., Grewal et al. 2009). Based on our findings, however, we extend the idea that

> customers consider value way beyond the pricing of the product and/or service in question.

We posit that customers do not evaluate an offering purely on the basis of the price. Customers' value perception of an offering includes other costs associated with the search and purchase process, such as time, effort, resources needed to purchase the offering in question, etc. (Klaus & Maklan, 2012). Value perceptions occur throughout all parts of the CX journey, prior, during, and after the purchase/use/consumption of the firm's offerings. For example, the influence of competitors is evident in the value perceptions of the brand, which is based on benchmarking the brand in question versus other competitors with which the customers have had direct or indirect interactions in the past. This "mental benchmarking" of experiences also influences the evaluations of direct interactions with the service provider and all of the company's channels. And while, as Grewal et al. (2009) state, it is "impossible to separate the effect of individual products, the entire assortment, (competition) and promotion on price (or value perceptions), or vice versa" (p. 5), EXQ delivers to a firm a clear understanding of what truly drives their customer behavior.

It can be measured after all ...

EXQ can be used by managers to determine which (CX) strategies and practices will have the most positive influence on their customers' perceptions and behavior. EXQ connects the customer's evaluation of the service in a more direct way than traditional key marketing scales, such as customer satisfaction and service quality, to loyalty, share-of-category, and word-of-mouth behavior. This allows firms to improve their CX management, and, finally, performance.

Measuring the customer experience is not only a, if not the, key driver of the most profitable CX strategies – the Vanguards – but it also displays why

being a Vanguard and measuring CX go hand-in-hand.

CX managers need to be concerned with improving the quality of the experiences they provide across all three dimensions of CX quality: *brand experience, service (firm) experience, and post-purchase/consumption experience*. These dimensions are key determinants of customer satisfaction, loyalty, and word-of-mouth behavior. Of the three EXQ dimensions, *post-purchase/ consumption experience* has the strongest influence on loyalty and word-of-mouth behavior. This emphasizes the need for firms to pay extra attention to this dimension, indicating that managing the CX must begin prior to, and cannot end until after, the purchase. Managers can succeed in developing effective CX strategies based upon EXQ's three pillars due to their significant influence on their customers' behavior. The corresponding CX management strategy will communicate the importance that the experiences have by focusing on all three dimensions of the customer experience and its temporal implications, and manage the customer experience prior to, during, and after the purchase and/or consumption of their offerings.

Due to the nature of CX – which is dependent not only on front-line employees, as the study reveals, but on all areas that contribute to the customer experience during all three stages – EXQ can only be practical, operational and reliable if the results are owned and accepted by all business functions (Reichheld 2003); that is, they are all responsible for delivering the experiences desired by their customers. EXQ builds a constant feedback loop for managers, allowing them to understand how their customers evaluate the different dimensions and attributes of their CX by linking them to important marketing outcomes.

> After all, a firm must first understand the triggers of this behavior

and its importance to the outcomes in order to improve its CX, establishing a close link to revenue (see Figure 7.3).

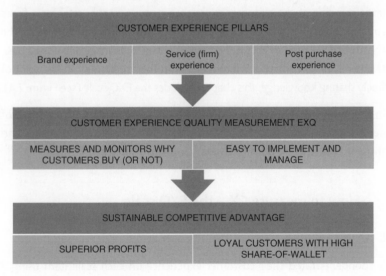

FIG 7.3 / **The power of EXQ**

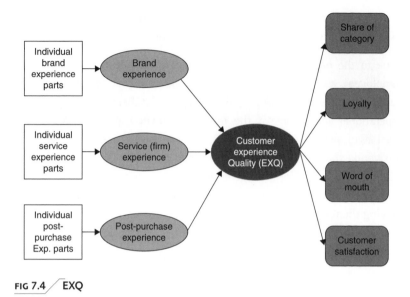

FIG 7.4 / **EXQ**

Because of its importance as a key determinant of customer satisfaction, loyalty, and word-of-mouth behavior, EXQ delivers even more evidence that managers need to consider CX as an important strategic objective. An understanding of the customer experience is, quite frankly, vital for a firm's strategic objectives and effective interactions with different customers. The construct developed by the study provides a way for managers to ensure positive behavior and behavioral intentions from their customers. In the spirit of freely sharing knowledge, this chapter includes the EXQ scale (see Figure 7.4).

In the following chapter, I will demonstrate, using evidence from some of our most recent studies, the currently best CX management practices and those in future using both EXQ and Vanguard strategy.

How to measure CX – the EXQ scale

EXQ

Respondents rated their customer experience on each scale item using a 7-point scale (1 = strongly disagree, 7 = strongly agree) or as Do not know/

Not applicable. The items below are grouped by dimensions for expositional convenience; they appeared in random order in the survey. The symbols preceding the items correspond to the variables named in Figure 7.1.

Brand experience
BRE1   XYZ has a good reputation.

BRE2   I am confident in XYZ's expertise.

BRE3   XYZ gives independent advice (on which product/service will best suit my needs).

BRE4   I choose XYZ not because of the price alone.

BRE5   The people who work at XYZ represent the XYZ brand well.

BRE6   XYZ's offerings have the best quality.

BRE7   XYZ's offerings are superior.

Service (provider) experience
SPE1   XYZ advised me throughout the process.

SPE2   Dealing with XYZ is easy.

SPE3   XYZ keeps me informed.

SPE4   XYZ demonstrates flexibility in dealing with me.

SPE5   At XYZ I always deal with the same forms and/or same people.

SPE6   XYZ's personnel relates to my wishes and concerns.

SPE7   The people I am dealing with [at XYZ] have good people skills.

SPE8   XYZ delivers a good customer service.

SPE9   I have built a personal relationship with the people at XYZ.

SPE10   XYZ's facilities are better designed to fulfill my needs than their competitors'.

SPE11   XYZ's online facilities are designed to be as efficient as possible (for me).

SPE12   XYZ's offline facilities are designed to be as efficient as possible (for me).

Post-purchase/consumption experience
PPE1   I stay with XYZ because they know me.

PPE2   XYZ knows exactly what I want.

PPE3   XYZ keeps me up-to-date.

PPE4   XYZ will look after me for a long time.

PPE5   XYZ deal(t) well with me when things go (went) wrong.

PPE6   I am happy with XYZ as my (service provider).

PPE7   Being a client at/customer of XYZ gives me social approval.

chapter 8

Best Practice vs. Next Practice

Faraway, but oh, so close

Let's reflect upon what we have covered up to this point. We have learned about the history of CX, CX strategies, and management practices. We have established CX as the next competitive battleground. Firms have no other strategic option – they need to engage in CX management. Nevertheless, there are different options available on how to manage CX, and we have established the three practices as being Preservers, Transformers, and Vanguards. These practices differ across all dimensions of CX management and, more importantly, achieve different amounts of profitability. Vanguards outperform the others by far, leading us to focus on their practices. We explored, using three examples, how each and every firm can develop a Vanguard strategy using a step-by-step approach. Next, we presented the most crucial factor in a firm's performance: the challenge of measuring the customer experience. We introduced EXQ as a comprehensive CX quality measurement, and established its superior explanatory and predictive powers.

Against this background, I will now demonstrate the hypothesized influence of the Internet on CX, substantiating this with the findings of our latest research. Then, using a real-world example, I will show how a company can move on from a Preserver strategy towards a Vanguard strategy, using EXQ as the "change agent."

The online experience

In only a few years, the Internet has established itself as a tool that has not only changed the way we communicate but also the way we do business. It is a true global communication medium that has evolved as the primary source of information for billions of people. In the last five years the user numbers have doubled worldwide, and for over 3 billion people the Internet is now a part of their lifestyle (International Telecommunications Union 2014). Online channels have changed the face of the business environment, influencing each and every industry and market. The digital age has arrived, and it is not only changing the way that customers make purchasing decisions, but also how firms do business. In the United States alone, nearly 50 percent of online customers are advanced users of smartphones, social networks, and other emerging tools (Kim & Ko 2012). This shift highlights changes in how customers use core technologies. Firms react to these customer behavior changes by progressively offering more and more sophisticated online tools to compete for contemporary and digitalized customers (Konus et al. 2008). Exploring the customer experience, in particular using online channels, is of increasing importance to firms worldwide (Verhoef et al. 2009). Previous studies indicate that the creation of compelling online experiences for web users will have numerous positive impacts for firms (Klaus 2013), but there is an urgent need for studies to explore how firms address the challenges of the new multi-channel CX environment (Neslin et al. 2006). Meanwhile, the majority of existing studies focus on the influence that these new technologies and subsequent channel choices have on customer behavior (e.g., Beldad et al. 2010).

Our research is grounded in the belief that we must first comprehend the practices of managing online retail channels through the eyes of the firm. Then we can examine what strategies optimize the firm's customer interaction, and what CX strategies have the most positive influence in terms of financial returns on customer online channel experiences over time (Hanssens et al. 2009). We investigated these things using the same approach as outlined in Chapters 4 and 5. The study confirmed, predictably, both, our existing CX strategy typology and its five dimension of CX management.

Some might see this as a revelation, because, after all, online channels are commonly referred to as the pathway to new customer behavior. I believe we can challenge this notion since

> technology is an enabler but not the focus and therefore driver of customer experience.

Customers are looking for a certain experience, and if online channels deliver this, they will act accordingly. Technology reflects nothing more than the customers' never-ending drive for fast, reliable, accommodating experiences tailored to their aims, tastes, and personal schedules, that is, when they want it and how they want it. Technologies can, or (allow me to rephrase) should, make the life of each and every customer easier. Vanguards' strategies demonstrate this practice and focus on technology as an enabler to deliver customer experiences at the exact points in time the customer desires them. Vanguards think holistically, acknowledging that in the end, in most cases, it is the human-to-human interaction that drives customer experience perception and customer behavior. While the crucial interaction is between human beings, technology can enable the design and execution of these interactions in an optimal way through, as discussed earlier, back-office and front-office integration, delivering all information right when it is needed to provide the best customer experience possible. With technology advancing, Vanguards focus on the common factors that drive customer experiences and behavior, using all available technology solely for its impact on customer behavior, as measured by, for example, EXQ.

Online? Offline? No, CX is multi-channel!

We focus on the Vanguard equivalent to illustrate their online and multi-channel CX practices. Vanguards, almost by definition, do not divide their practices between online and offline; they concede that all channels count, and therefore, even if their business is based upon an e-commerce model, always refer to a multi-channel strategy. They possess a clear strategic model of multi-channel CX management that is visible throughout the firm and in the matching business processes and practices. Vanguards have an even greater emphasis on integrating and amalgamating all functions and channels to implement best practices throughout the firm and partner businesses. Vanguards noticeably connect multi-channel practice, outcomes, and goals as defined and controlled by a central function or division, encompassing multiple organizational functions. Vanguards use online channels – social media in particular – to gain customer insight, conduct training, monitor project management, decide upon resource allocation, and develop human resources. Vanguards' practices center on a relentless refinement of their multi-channel business model, based upon internal research and implemented by all functions throughout the firm.

Financial services are a prime example of how important the customer experience has become. Researchers often suggest that financial services require a customer's important, complex, and considered choice, with a long purchase process containing numerous service episodes. Considered purchases are likely to display customer experience as a key determinant of customer retention (Sharma & Patterson 1999). Financial planning services are also often complex (Sharma & Patterson 2000), customized, and high in credence properties. In the past, financial services customer management practices focused on customer satisfaction, and its suggested precursor, service quality. Service quality is a gap between customers' expectations and their overall assessment (perceptions) of the service encounter (Parasuraman et al. 1988). As we pointed out earlier, this popular gap concept led to the widespread management motto of needing to "delight" customers by always exceeding their expectations. Even today, some managers and consultants declare that their firm's sole function is to delight their customers. While I admit that this proposition has a certain allure, financially, as research points out,

Considered purchases are likely to display customer experience as a key determinant of customer retention

> delighting the customer can force a firm into bankruptcy.

The same is true about customer satisfaction. In a recent article, colleagues of mine declare that ill-advised attempts to improve satisfaction for the sake of increasing their customer satisfaction score can damage a company's financial health (Keiningham et al. 2041). In some cases, their research points out, it might even be obligatory to accept lower average satisfaction levels in the pursuit of greater market share by attracting a larger, less uniform customer base. This challenges the message of many programs discussed in the popular business press regarding the relationship of satisfaction (and NPS) to business performance (Keiningham et al. 2007). Thus, a growing satisfaction level could be a helpful item for the firm's overall strategy, but it doesn't have to be. As my colleagues put it so eloquently,

> often customer satisfaction isn't compatible with market share growth – or even good business.

According to one of our most recent studies (Ponsignon et al. 2014), financial services seem to be one of the industry sectors that are already executing CX strategies based on the opposite of delighting customers. Their practices revolve around avoiding bad customer experiences rather than trying to "wow" them. By investigating the last (on average) five years of 20 financial services organizations in detail, using our typology we looked at Vanguard practices. The key components of Vanguards in financial services and their management practices support our typology, but there are some striking similarities in terms of what they consider key components of the CX practices. All Vanguards describe their CX strategy as based on a continuum (see Klaus et al. 2013). Vanguard firms use this continuum notion to model CX touch-points and stages maps. These stages are mostly generic, but firms develop detailed CX maps at a more granular level for each main product line. For instance, an insurance company produced a different model for each of its three main savings products (i.e., life cover; tax-exempt savings plans, and bonds). Financial services firms differentiate between the concepts of "product" and "process," and create process and experience designs according to their customer requirements. CX management is, therefore, an extension of, and embedded in, the end-to-end process design. Based upon this CX practice, firms identify and select improvement opportunities, with the emphasis on locating under-performing moments of truths, often referred to as fail, break, or pain points. A break point is a critical encounter that consistently attracts negative feedback from customers. It is associated with an increase in customer pain and has an adverse effect on key customer outcomes. Thus, firms allocate resources to improving failed moments of truth. In summary, the focus is on avoiding bad experiences. In the following section I will introduce an example of how all these components are used to move towards the most profitable CX strategies. It's a story that demonstrates how to become a Vanguard.

How to overcome the challenges – an illustration

In today's economy, the multi-channel business model increasingly becomes the prevalent one. Many firms today are struggling to come to a consensus on how to move towards a successful (multi-channel) CX strategy. Our studies detail the tensions (between departments, functions, different stakeholders) that firms have to first overcome in order to succeed with a CX strategy that is accepted company-wide. Once this has been achieved, firms face the task of managing the CX transformation internally. We encourage firms to overcome their "silo" challenges and adopt a holistic view of how all channels can contribute to the customer experience and organizational success.

In the following, I want to share with you an example of how a financial service group used EXQ as a "Trojan horse" to move their CX strategy towards becoming a Vanguard.

I was approached by the retail banking division of a financial services firm, which was eager to explore recent hard-to-explain movements in their customer base, about my customer experience quality scale. During initial conversations with the board members, we presented the capabilities of EXQ and the business case for CX, which led to us undertaking a project with the firm. In brief, we built a CX construct based on the EXQ model (Klaus & Maklan 2012; Klaus et al. 2013). We agreed to limit the investigation to the drivers of customer behavior in order to consider a set of actionable variables from a management standpoint. We measured the perceptions of the firm's retail customers qualitatively (20 customers) and quantified the findings with 325 customers. The EXQ measurement development process (see Chapter 7) confirmed EXQ and its three dimensions (brand experience, service experience, and post-purchase experience) and CX's positive and significant influence on customer satisfaction, loyalty, and word-of-mouth behavior.

The results, demonstrating the key drivers of customer behavior, presented several vital findings that were particularly useful for designing an effective strategy to overcome the current business hurdle.

1. *Customers make decisions based upon a CX continuum, and not on single encounters.*
   We demonstrated that all direct and indirect company–customer interactions are crucial during the pre-purchase, purchase, and post-purchase phases. Customers expect high levels of service from the firm during all moments of contact with it. Subsequently, actions that aim to improve only one particular step, touch-point, or interaction are insufficient to deliver the experiences customers desire. The management understood the risk involved in relying on insight from traditional customer quality and satisfaction measures. Every direct and indirect interaction with the firm affects the customers' perception of quality and, therefore, it is important to improve all interactions as parts of a *continuum*.

2. *Customize marketing actions to the customer's state.*

Measuring EXQ provides the firm with the ability to attune their actions according to specific phases in a customer's purchasing process. The firm realized this afforded the opportunity to deliver the right action at the right moment. For instance, if a customer is in the pre-purchase stage, the firm should deliver messages to enhance the most important perceptions corresponding to this stage, such as guarantees and delivering independent advice. Customers in the purchasing stage require different experiences, such as the flexibility and expertise of personnel. In the post-purchasing phase the firm needs to acknowledge the importance of future transactions over the whole customer life cycle. Incorrect alignments between these actions and customers' stages in the process will lead to unfavorable customer behavior and an ensuing inferior performance.

3. *Integrate different organizational units.*

All organizational units contribute to how customers make decisions,

hence the need to be integrated into an overarching (CX) program. Often, different teams or units manage customers at different stages. For example, we identified that decisions related to the pre-purchase phase are highly influenced by the firm's marketing activities. Customer-facing personnel are the key contact points for customers in the purchasing stage, while customer service officers deal with problems arising in the post-purchase phase. Although it is obviously important to let the firm's organizational units specialize in their respective competence areas, designing an effective CX strategy definitely requires integrating the efforts of all staff members in dealing with customers and making individual units aware of a customer's current stage and the corresponding experiences required.

4. *Allocate the marketing and communication budgets according to the customer's individual CX stage.*

CX improvement budgets need to be allocated according to customers' individual stages. Our data analysis revealed that the service experience

during a transaction is the main driver in explaining how customers assess their experience. EXQ provides the bank with
Based on these results, the firm assessed its marketing and communication budget allocation.

a quantitative evaluation of the relative importance of individual factors.

5. *Measure the effects of actions on CX and improve the strategy accordingly.*
We suggest measuring EXQ constantly in a longitudinal way, which would allow firms to monitor the effectiveness of their actions and, if necessary, take corrective actions.

The results are in ...

Based upon our findings, the firm used our findings to implement multiple changes. In the first instance, the findings and their importance were communicated openly throughout the entire firm. In particular, the CX continuum idea was used as a key message. EXQ, and its quantified ability to measure CX's tremendous influence on customer satisfaction, loyalty, and word-of-mouth, is the change agent that leads the transformation towards a CX Vanguard strategy. In addition, the entire marketing communication was amended to both use the insight gained from EXQ and highlight the importance of CX at each stage. In a subsequent stage, the firm is now introducing an entire new branch system, based on their EXQ-driven, constantly developing CX strategy.

This is an excellent example of how a business challenge triggered an openness to explore the key drivers of customer behavior. In my experience, business challenges involving customer insight or the lack thereof (e.g., a customer churn without any visible explanation, less-than-expected growth despite high customer satisfaction rating, or bad reviews online), are not an uncommon occurrence. All of these challenges provide an excellent opportunity to enter the next competitive battleground – customer experience – and develop the most profitable strategies. We discussed some of the internal and external hurdles firms have to overcome in order to implement change. And, let's be quite honest, developing a Vanguard CX strategy, by definition, is a change process on an all-encompassing level. Humans are by default resistant to change. Consequently, rather than trying to convince all stakeholders that a Vanguard CX strategy is the way to go, we can learn from the financial services firm's case, and deploy a "Trojan horse" approach. Given the fact that measuring the customer experience is a key pillar of the most profitable CX practices, you are already moving in the right direction. However, rather than encountering possible resistance, you are managing, (i.e. delivering insight and solutions for mastering a business challenge). Once your colleagues see the evidence and acumen EXQ delivers, the process of using a measurement to initiate change will be significantly less laborious. In addition, the individual attributes and requirements will be based on the drivers of customer behavior, and therefore profitability, rather than on some other agenda. This fact, too, in my experience, will facilitate the willingness to participate and better embrace a CX program. EXQ delivers, quite simply, a clear business case for CX management. An alternative approach to successfully pave the way for a CX strategy is the following five-step model.

1. Use a managerial/business challenge for a "call to action."
2. Exploit EXQ as the means to deliver "hard evidence" of what truly drives customer behavior, and, therefore profitability.
3. Convert the insights gained from EXQ into managerial actions.
4. Develop the business case for CX through accountable and quantifiable results.
5. Gain support and move towards becoming a Vanguard, based on the EXQ's explanatory and predictive powers.

People change and so does their CX evaluation

There is yet another reason why measuring CX is so important in developing, implementing, and managing a successful CX strategy. We know that customers' CX perceptions and evaluations often develop over a series of interactions, and purchasing and consumption episodes with the firm. Some offerings, such as services, often require customers to engage with the firm multiple times over an extended period of time. These experiences are dynamic in nature, and managers need to understand how the customers' needs change as their interactions with the organization progress (Dagger and Sweeney 2007). An understanding of the underlying triggers of these changes is even more significant to the firm, given the importance of increasing customer retention and loyalty (Zeithaml 2000) and building long-term profitable relationships with their customers (Verhoef 2003).

Researchers pay much attention to the dynamic development of customer satisfaction (e.g., Bolton & Drew 1991; Boulding et al. 1993; Mittal et al. 1999). These studies usually use longitudinal data on customer satisfaction from the same group of customers. These studies suggest two important things: (1) current customer satisfaction affects future expectations; and (2) current satisfaction scores are strong predictors of future satisfaction scores. This means that satisfaction scores are pretty stable over time and that there are strong carry-over effects. However, some critical incidents can trigger an updating process in which new information (from the critical incidents) is included in the customers' assessments (e.g., Bolton 1998; van Doorn & Verhoef 2008). Similar phenomena might occur for customers' experience evaluations. Phenomena similar to these satisfaction-updating processes may well occur in the broader domain of customer experience as well. This leads to important questions, such as the following: Are CX triggers – and the nature and extent of their effects – stable over time? Do customers expect an increasingly positive customer experience over time? And might customers (to some extent) become "bored with" or accustomed to the delivered experience, and will the experience vary between, for example, first, repeat, and regular customers? Using EXQ, the firm can answer these questions by constantly monitoring possible shifts in which of the CX triggers influence behavior most. Based upon my research, I propose that measuring EXQ frequently will deliver not only answers to these questions, but allow managers to

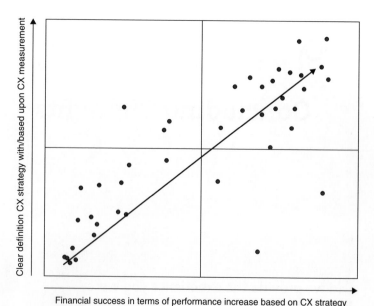

FIG 8.1 / **Measuring CX drives superior performance**

develop adaptive foresight. No, I am not referring to a crystal ball, but by using sophisticated statistical methods, firms not only can monitor possible shifts in their customers' CX assessment, but also can model how these changes will occur in the future. This gives firms a powerful tool to design the desired customer experience for each customer exactly when they desire it, thereby being proactive, and, consequently, based on what we have already established, maximizing profitability (see Figure 8.1).

chapter 9

Concluding Thoughts

Did we provide the experience you were looking for?

It's time to reflect and ask, "Did *Measuring Customer Experience* deliver (the experience) I was looking for?" We started by stating that we are entering the CX age – an era where customers call the shots and success will be based on how well firms can rise to meet customer demands and expectations. Only firms that deliver desired customer experiences will survive in the next competitive battleground. But how can this be achieved?

- by clearly defining CX. What is it exactly?
- What influence does it have on a firm's performance?
- How can it be measured?
- How can it be managed?
- And, if it can be managed, which strategies are the most profitable ones?

Measuring Customer Experience promises answers to these crucial questions, and delivers. It clearly defines the CX phenomenon and delivers unique insights into the history and evolution of CX. It defines CX from a managerial viewpoint and uses a global study to clearly define CX and its management practices from a firm's viewpoint. Next, it connects these practices to profitability, indicating which strategies are the most profitable ones. Based upon these insights, *Measuring Customer Experience* gives examples of how to move step-by-step towards the most profitable CX strategies. It delivers a CX measurement, one of the most crucial challenges for all firms – EXQ. Combining all these insights, *Measuring Customer Experience* demonstrates different options for embarking on the journey towards becoming a Vanguard, for example, by using EXQ as a "Trojan horse."

I can share with you that the first question posed by managers after being exposed to our research findings is "How can I become a Vanguard?" This is a very good question indeed, and if I had to summarize the essence of *Measuring Customer Experience* I would advise you to take the following steps in order to design profitable CX strategies:

1. Establish your "status quo" and draw a strategic roadmap for becoming a *Vanguard*.
   Our typology of CX strategies and management practices allows you to establish current and desired states. This allows firms to draw a roadmap of how to implement and execute their new strategy on all levels of CX management and, in the process, develop corresponding practices and capabilities.

2. Focus CX strategy on a continuum, and not on single encounters.
   Every direct and indirect interaction with the firm affects the customer's perception of quality. Therefore, it is important to improve all interactions as parts of a *continuum* (Klaus et al. 2013).

3. Integrate all organizational units.
   All organizational units contributing to the customer experience need to be integrated into the CX program. Often, different teams or units manage customers at different stages.

4. Measure the effects of actions on CX in a dynamic fashion.
   Anchor your CX strategy around measuring EXQ constantly in a longitudinal way. This will allow you to monitor the effectiveness of your

CX practices proactively and take advantage of the explanatory and predictive power of EXQ.

Allow me also to share some of the most common questions we encounter when discussing the challenges of CX management practice (you might have some similar ones).

1. Are there any particular, context-specific challenges in designing and executing successful CX strategies?
   Of course, by definition, every so often there will be context-specific challenges. Based on the evidence from our studies, though, I can confidently state that *Measuring Customer Experience* delivers answers on how to master the most common and frequently occurring challenges.

2. Can all companies become Vanguards, and, if so, is this desirable or even appropriate?
   In theory, all firms should be able to become Vanguards if they have both the capability and commitment required to succeed in this change. In practice, not everyone can or wants to become a Vanguard. There may be circumstances when becoming a Vanguard might not be the best option. As a child I learned that there are no rules without exception, and this applies to CX strategies too. If your firm's desire is to enter the next competitive battleground – customer experience –you might not even have the opportunity to opt out of this decision; however, if your firm is set on developing the most profitable CX strategies and management practices, you shouldn't waste any time trying to become a Vanguard. Even if you don't succeed completely, every step towards becoming a Vanguard can make your firm more profitable, so why wouldn't you try? *Measuring Customer Experience* delivers evidence for ways to succeed in this endeavor, but if you are uncertain

about anything, just get in touch with me and hopefully I'll be able to provide you with even more of the tools you might need.

3. Can companies evolve, say, from being a Transformer to becoming a Vanguard?
   Yes, they can, and we have discussed examples in detail. It is possible, and I hope you will embark on this exciting journey.

4. What is the best way to initiate or change a company's CX strategy?
   There isn't really a best way, because the circumstances will differ from firm to firm. One proven way to initiate these changes is by linking CX strategy to performance, and using a CX measurement such as EXQ is a verified way to do this. After all, only what gets measured gets managed.

On a personal note, please allow me to express my gratitude and say thank you for taking the time to read my book, I hope you had a good experience and found some answers to the questions that were on your mind. I hope that by now you comprehend that I am rather passionate about customer experience and the challenges it brings to firms, managers, consultants, and researchers. I believe it is my duty, and pleasure to explore CX, CX strategies, and CX management in order to share the knowledge we create with everyone who is interested. This passion and my thirst for knowledge drive my research and my ambitions to deliver information that you can use to make your firm a better performing one using CX – after all, successful CX is based upon delivering great experiences. Thus, if we all get the experiences we are looking for, we are happy – at least that's what I believe. And what more can one wish for than being (partially) responsible for another person's happiness?

Being well aware that the post-purchase experience is crucial in influencing both your experience and your assessment of it, I want to provide you with some free additional resources that you might find useful (please see page xxx for details).

I believe that we all learn something new every single day, and I would love you to share your invaluable insight and feedback on my book and our research with me.

Please contact me at profdrphilklaus@gmail.com.

Your consideration is highly appreciated and I am looking forward to hearing from you.

Yours sincerely

Prof. Dr. Phil Klaus

Free resources aka SWAG

Definition of SWAG – A slang term used to describe free stuff and givea-ways offered by vendors at trade shows to encourage attendees to visit their stand. Swag is usually company-branded merchandise and is given away as a form of advertising. SWAG can also be obtained through blogs and websites when a company wants to promote their brand or products.

- Gain free access to most of our articles @ www.profdrphilklaus.com
- Follow us on Twitter @profdrphilklaus
- Join The Customer Experience Agenda, and gain complimentary access to cutting-edge research for businesses from the world's top scholars on LinkedIn. http://tinyurl.com/marketingscholarsonLinkedIn
- Check the interviews with CX Thought leaders on our Youtube Channel http://tinyurl.com/CX-Strategy
- Receive a free strategy evaluation of your CX strategy (including bench-marking) by following http://tinyurl.com/Measure-CX-Evaluation

chapter 10

The Science behind the Knowledge

Very often managers ask me if they can simply use data they have already collected in order to move towards becoming a Vanguard or to measure customer experience. While I understand the allure that existing data has in terms of immediate availability and no added costs, the shortcomings of the data outweigh any possible benefits. It's quite simple: if you don't ask the right questions in order to develop a Vanguard strategy or measure customer experience, the answers will be a poor fit for the challenges you are trying to address. Retrofitting data and insight is not recommended and can also be counterproductive to the firm's aim of developing long-term profitability. Don't get me wrong – the data and resulting insights you already have are valuable. However, the data need to be used at the right time and in the right place. In most cases the firms we encounter are perfectly able to determine what their customers are doing. Moreover, firms gain insight on how and when their customers act, and how these actions can be stimulated. But while what and how are answered perfectly, the missing insight is often why customers act (or do not) act in a particular way. Without the why, the what, how, and when make very little sense. Answering the why questions requires a different set of research skills, patience, and a lon-gitudinal view on how to gain insight. Exploratory,

without the why, the what, how, and when make very little sense

qualitative, longitudinal research using insights from psychology isn't often used in the fast-paced business environment. In particular, in the holistic CX management domain, the complexity – the nature of the beast – can only be converted into actions and results if the right methods are chosen right from the start. Developing a measurement of CX quality is a prime example. In our 2011 and 2013 *International Journal of Marketing Research* articles we described the complexity of the issue in detail. In our article asking if market researchers were using the right measures to help their firms improve customer experience, we established that customer experience was conceptually different from service quality and hence requires a new corresponding measurement (Klaus & Maklan 2007). The role of measurement in successfully implementing and executing strategy is long established and well documented (e.g., Martilla & James 1977). This role is particularly crucial for new emerging paradigm shifts (Bowden 2009) such as the most recent one towards CX management (Smith 2002).

Based on research and literature, we defined customer experience as the customer's cognitive and affective assessment of all direct and indirect encounters with the firm relating to their purchasing behavior. This establishes the crucial link between CX and profitability, as outlined throughout all the chapters.

In this chapter I explain in detail the science behind the EXQ scale used to measure customer behavior based upon their experiences. I believe this will benefit readers who are interested in having more background information about how we developed our insight, and that it can assist you in developing similar CX insight programs.

It's complex, but worth it … developing a CX scale

Dear reader, please be kind enough to note that the following description of the procedures and processes is based on one example, and is written in technical, academic language.

This study presents a validated multi-item scale based on the underlying construct of CX and extends previous research on CX and service quality measures. The measure is called the CX quality scale, EXQ. The research determines its dimensions by analyzing what customers describe as the triggers of their purchasing and repurchasing behaviors. The authors conducted exploratory research to develop a new multi-dimensional consumer-based CX quality scale based on customers' service experiences. The methodology follows Churchill's (1979) scale-development paradigm. The scale is, as suggested by other scale-development studies (e.g., Brocato et al. 2012, Walsh & Beatty 2007), developed in four stages: scale generation, purification, reliability and validity assessment, and establishment of further discriminate validity (see Figure 7.2).

Stage 1 articulates the meaning and domain of the CX, based on insights from the literature and a comprehensive qualitative study. It results in a preliminary scale containing 48 items representing three dimensions.

Stage 2 describes the administration of the scale to representative samples of the contexts chosen for this study, namely: North American customers of lifestyle luxury apparel retail services, wealth management services, retail banking services and customers of fuel and service stations, from a total of 600 completed questionnaires (150 questionnaires per sample). Using exploratory factor analysis, the scale is purified to 25 items that represent three CX quality dimensions.

Stage 3 validates the purified scale using CFA based on 200 collected questionnaires from representative samples of each context – a total of 800 questionnaires, which confirms the scale's reliability and validity.

Stage 4 introduces the final scale and the conceptual framework of CX, relating it to important marketing outcomes, as suggested by Brown et al. (2005); Dagger et al. (2007); Parasuraman et al. (2005); Walsh & Beatty (2007); and Zeithaml et al. (1996). In addition, EXQ's explanatory power in relationship to these outcomes is compared with the prevalent measurement of service quality, SERVQUAL (e.g., Buttle 1996).

Stage 1: The qualitative study

To articulate the meaning and the domain of CX and its measure, the initial stage of the research explores the perceptual attributes of CX quality through in-depth interviews using the soft laddering technique (Grunert and Grunert 1995; Botschen et al. 1999). Soft laddering is a technique using personal in-depth interviews where respondents are restricted as little as possible in their natural flow of speech, and it is an accepted method for assessing consumers' cognitive structures and underlying purchasing motivations (Reynolds et al. 1995).

While some marketing scholars create awareness of the context-specific nature of the CX (e.g., Lemke et al. 2011), the aim of our research is to develop a CX quality scale on the theoretical foundations laid out in the literature review in order to be readily adapted to different types of retail service firms. In order to develop a CX quality scale capable of serving this purpose, we adapted and extended the reliable and validated Silvestro et al.'s (1992) service classification scheme (e.g., Auzair & Langfield-Smith 2005). Subsequently, we chose one professional service (wealth management: Hussain & Chong 2008), one mass service (fuel and service station: Jones 2008), and one service shop (retail banking: Silvestro 1999). In addition, we included service reflecting the hedonic nature of CXs (lifestyle luxury goods retail). The latter service was chosen to ensure further cross-validation (Cronin et al. 2000), so that samples varied in the degree to which the service could be characterized as hedonic (lifestyle luxury goods) versus utilitarian (fuel and service station).

Generating an initial item pool through qualitative research can be accomplished, according to Churchill (1979, p. 67), with an experience survey conducted with "a judgment sample of persons who can offer some ideas and insights into the phenomenon." The objective is to create an initial pool of items, which are then scrutinized thoroughly through other tests. We identified potential expert candidates for our study by following the procedure advocated by the literature, based on the following criteria (e.g., Hora & von Winterfeldt, 1997): (a) tangible evidence of expertise; (b) reputation; (c) availability and willingness to participate; (d) understanding of the general problem area; (e) impartiality; and (f) lack of an economic or personal stake in the potential findings. The respondents commented on all experiences and interactions encountered in the process of searching, evaluating, purchasing and/or using and consuming the offering in question. Thus, despite having a relationship with the current firm, respondents were able to comment on and describe their experiences prior to becoming a customer of the firm in question.

We achieved data saturation (Glaser & Strauss 1967) after conducting individual in-depth interviews with customers, according to the context in question as follows:

Wealth management clients: We conducted 20 interviews with customers from North America over a two-week period; each interview lasted between 30 and 60 minutes. The sample consisted of customers who had used the offered wealth service in the previous six months with one major US bank. The split between first-time buyers and repeat buyers was ten each. Customers were recruited by a market research company and offered a $100 incentive for their participation. The sample was randomly selected from amongst the clients of that bank.

Fuel and service station customers: We conducted 20 interviews with North American customers over a one-week period; each interview lasted between 30 and 45 minutes. The sample consisted of customers who held a loyalty card with the fuel and service station firm. Customers were recruited by a market research company and offered a cash equivalent of $50 for their participation. The sample was randomly selected from amongst the loyalty cardholders of the service firm.

Retail banking customers: We conducted 20 interviews with North American customers over a two-week period; each interview lasted between 20 and 50 minutes. The sample consisted of customers who in the previous six months had opened an account with one major US bank. The split between first-time buyers and repeat buyers was ten each. Customers were recruited by a market research company and offered a $50 incentive for their participation. The sample was randomly selected from amongst the customers of that bank.

Luxury goods customers: We conducted 25 interviews with customers from North America over a four-week period; each interview lasted between 20 and 40 minutes. The sample consisted of customers who purchased one or more luxury items during the six months prior to the interview.

Customers were recruited by a market research company and offered a cash equivalent incentive of US$50 for their participation. The sample was randomly selected from the customer database of the service firm.

Dimensions of customer experience scale and item generation

The interviews were transcribed and coded with the support of NVivo 8.0. The software enables the author to reflect on the key themes and to code and compare the data (Di Gregorio 2000; Clisbee 2003). Coding follows the grounded approach described by Ryan and Bernard (2003), which draws heavily from Strauss and Corbin (1990). The primary researchers incorporated independently a systematic and far-out comparison approach and hierarchical coding to ensure that we observed all the data thoroughly and explored all its dimensions (Strauss & Corbin 1990). The initial categorization of all attributes was the outcome of three extended workshops involving the primary researchers. Each attribute was named and defined. To warrant inclusion, an item had to be found in at least one interview. In a subsequent stage, researchers discussed differences in their attribute categorization and agreed on revised attributes and category definitions. Some constructs appeared in more than one interview. The researchers examined transcriptions and individual codes to identify such repetitions and define standardized construct names, resulting in a coherent coding structure. Based on these interviews and as a result of these purification workshops, the researchers generated 72 CX items out of an initial pool of 131.

Four marketing academics unfamiliar with the details of the research project and five customers per context assessed the readability of the items. To maximize the content and face validity of the items generated from the exploratory research, a panel of expert judges reviewed the retained item pool (Dagger et al. 2007). The expert panel comprised five marketing academics familiar with the scale-development process. The expert panel members performed three tasks.

1. The expert panel commented on the clarity, conciseness, and labeling of the items. Panel members were asked about the similarity of items, the clarity of phrasing, and the terminology used in the scale. This resulted in 22 items being removed or merged with other items. For example,

the items "Inertia" and "Convenience Retention" were merged into one item labeled "Convenience Retention."

2. The panel members then rated each of the 50 remaining items with respect to its relevance to the item description. Ratings were given on a 7-point scale, anchored by 1 = not at all representative, and 7 = strongly representative. Item purification began with the exclusion of any item rated by the panel members as either a 1 or a 2 on the rating scale. Three members of the panel had to rate the item as a 6 or 7 on the rating scale for an item to be included in the final scale. The panel removed eight items in the process.

3. The panel members were asked what dimensions evolved from the research model and items. Using the Q-sort technique (Funder et al. 2000), each item in the initial pool was printed on an index card, and each panel member was asked to create dimensions and sub-dimensions based on the similarity-representing aspect of the CX. It was up to the members to decide on the number of categories they used and to find appropriate labels and descriptions of the categories. The proportion of agreement among the judges was high, demonstrating high reliability. The Spearman correlation coefficient between judges was $r = 0.93$, $p < 0.05$.

The sorting procedure (Moore & Benbasat 1999) generated three categories of CX with 42 items. Two items were dropped because a number of judges identified them as being too ambiguous to fit into the emerging categories.

Finally, five marketing academics familiar with the research were given the conceptual description of the three dimensions and asked to rate the 42 items as either "very applicable," "somewhat applicable," or "not applicable" relative to the respective dimension. Items needed to be rated at least as "somewhat applicable" to be retained. This procedure resulted in retaining all 42 items and three dimensions.

The three dimensions representing 42 items are brand experience, service (firm) experience, and post-purchase/consumption experience.

Brand experience comprises brand perceptions influencing the CX (Fitzsimons et al. 2008) and the decision process of the customer (Mantrala et al. 2009). Brand experience reflects customers' value perception of products, pricing, the "experience-delivering" personnel, the brand, and competitors' offerings in the search process of evaluating offerings (e.g., Hoch 2002). It includes attributes of the social environment, such as reference groups and reviews (e.g., Luo 2005).

Service (firm) experience encompasses three themes associated with the experiences customers encounter when they interact with a firm's physical presence, personnel, policies, and practices (Brakus et al. 2009). The first theme relates to the process experience, including items such as process ease and the challenge of using multiple channels in dealing with the firm (Lemke et al. 2011). The second theme relates to direct evaluations of encounters with personnel, such as common grounding or the existence of personal relationships with the personnel (Grace & O'Cass 2004). The third theme describes the influence of the physical environment, such as Servicescape (Bitner 1992). The fourth theme relates to what researchers consider situational and consumer moderators, such as task orientation and location (e.g., Dabholkar & Bagozzi 2002).

Post-purchase/consumption experience describes the customers' experiences encountered post-purchase and consumption of the offering in question (Payne et al. 2008). One could argue that the product-in-use assessment might be difficult for customers such as first-time buyers of a wealth management service. However, the dimension focuses on all post-purchase consumption, not just product-in-use. It covers perceptions of familiarity (Söderlund 2002), retention (Verhoef 2003), and service recovery (Kelley & Davis 1994), displaying signs of customer commitment to the service firm (Bansal et al. 2004). The dimension also includes expressions of emotions associated with social and hedonic value, referring to post-purchase pleasure and an increase in social status based on the relationship with the service firm (e.g., Sweeney & Soutar 2001).

In summary, the qualitative study shows that consumers' conceptions of CX are aligned with the concept of CX we developed from prior research and theoretical writings in various disciplines.

The findings suggest CX can be defined as a holistic construct (Verhoef et al. 2009), including determinants such as social interactions (Bagozzi

2000), price (Baker et al. 2002), brand (Brodie et al. 2006), and channels (Payne & Frow 2005). The validity of the findings is scrutinized in the subsequent quantitative data analysis as outlined in Figure 7.2.

Stage 2: Scale purification through EFA

The scale was purified through a subsequent phase of quantitative research conducted amongst repeat purchasers: EFA. Data were collected as follows:

Wealth management clients – an online questionnaire accessible through a link sent by a market research firm to a sample of customers of a bank who had purchased the most services/products within the previous six months.

Fuel and service station customers – an online questionnaire accessible through a link sent by a market research firm to a sample of customers in their customer database.

Retail banking customers – an online questionnaire accessible through a link sent by a market research firm to a sample of customers in their customer database.

North American luxury goods customers – an online questionnaire accessible through a link sent by a market research firm to a sample of customers who had purchased items with the service firm within the previous three months.

The data test the appropriateness of the 48 items for generating the above three dimensions of CX, hence refining the scale. The corresponding survey generated 600 qualified responses (150 responses per context), which were subsequently analyzed utilizing the software packages SPSS 16.0 and AMOS 16.0.

Appendix A contains descriptive profiles of the exploratory stage of each context. The samples are analogous and a χ^2 test revealed that the samples do not differ significantly in terms of age, gender, educational background, and household income, allowing us to pool the samples for data analysis. We tested for non-response bias (Hudson et al. 2004) using an accepted procedure comparing early versus late responses (Armstrong & Overton 1977). We found no evidence of differences between the two, and we proceeded to conduct further tests prior to conducting the exploratory factor analysis. We consulted four tests to assess the suitability of the data for factor analysis. The Bartlett Test of Sphericity tested the overall significance of the correlation matrix and we used the Kaiser-Meyer-Olkin (KMO) measure of sampling adequacy to establish the suitability of the data for factor analysis (Tabachnick & Fidell 1996; Hair et al. 2009). The correlation matrix was examined to ensure that inter-item correlations were substantial (>0.30) and the anti-image matrix was assessed for low values (Hair et al. 2009). The Catell scree plot was also used as a diagnostic indicator for factor extraction. As the factors are expected to be correlated, we obliquely rotated the factors using the direct oblimin procedure (Polit 1996; Hair et al. 2009). The results of the factor analysis were assessed in conjunction with the results from scale reliability analysis using Cronbach's alpha and item-to-total correlations. In the analysis process, 17 items were eliminated due to high cross-loadings, insufficient values on the anti-image matrix, and their item-to-total correlation. The 17 items were as follows: best rate/price; price sensitivity; peer-to-peer interactions; experience with other firms; promotions; reviews; product variety; store location; process frustration; freedom of choice; buying/shopping purpose; customization; convenience; control; feeling appreciated; loyalty benefits; and improvement of self-perception. Our approach of sequentially eliminating items with low loadings on all factors, or high cross-loading on two or more factors, followed by factor analysis of the remaining items, has been used in widely cited analogous scale-development studies (Parasuraman et al. 2005). The number of items dropped after the purification stage is not necessarily an indicator that a unique part of the latent variable is missing (Klaus & Maklan 2012). This is supported by our analysis, namely: the remaining data pass the threshold for sampling adequacy; KMO MSA 0.891 passes Bartlett's test of sphericity significance with 0.000, displays a substantial inter-item correlation, and generates acceptable values on the anti-image matrix. The scree plot suggests a factoring of 25 items in three dimensions, explaining 85.3 percent of all variances. A Cronbach alpha factor of 0.882, and the fact that each of the remaining items of the scale EXQ displays an item-total correlation of at least 0.751, support the validity and reliability of the scale. As suggested by marketing researchers (e.g., Zeithaml et al. 1996), demographic profiles of the respondent samples were reviewed by managers in the respective companies and were considered to be representative of their customer bases.

The purpose of the EFA is to summarize the data into a minimum number of factors for prediction purposes. The resulting purified scale (see Table 7.1) posits CX quality as comprising three primary dimensions, with 25 corresponding items developed to operationalize each of these dimensions. The resulting three dimensions and corresponding items were presented to four marketing academics familiar with the research. The expert panel was given the conceptual description of the three dimensions and asked to rate the three dimensions' description as either "very applicable," "somewhat applicable," or "not applicable," relative to the dimension and its items. Dimension descriptions needed to be rated as at least "somewhat applicable" to be retained. This procedure resulted in the labeling of the three dimensions of CX, namely:

1. Brand experience.
2. Service (firm) experience.
3. Post-purchase/consumption experience.

After purification, 25 items in three dimensions remained. The resulting purified scale of CX quality EXQ is given in Table 7.1. We noted that certain attributes suggested by researchers as being a part of the CX proved to be statistically irrelevant. We will put forward possible explanations for these findings in our discussion section.

Stage 3: Reliability and validity assessment of measure

Next, we conducted CFA to assess further the factor structure of the EXQ scale. To perform the analysis we collected an additional sample per context. Data were collected through the same means as described earlier for EFA, and a total of 800 (200 per context) qualified responses were collected. The response rate for this and the previous stage were between

19.4 percent and 28.7 percent, higher than those reported in similar consumer studies (e.g., Parasuraman et al. 1994). Respondents rated their CX on each scale item using a 7-point scale (1 = *Strongly disagree*, 7 = *Strongly agree*) or as Do not know/Not applicable. We grouped the items by dimensions for expositional convenience; they appeared in random order on the survey. The symbols preceding the items corresponded to the variables named in Table 7.1 (see Appendix B).

Prior to data analysis, a preliminary preparation of the data was conducted as outlined in Stage 2. In order to verify the factor structure and dimensionality of the refined scale, researchers needed to collect a sufficient number of responses. According to Hair et al. (2009), the sample size required to conduct CFA is five observations per scale item. Thus, the sample size for the validation stage of the study exceeded the requirements to achieve a high level of statistical power.

Before running the structural model, we examined whether the four samples could be pooled or demanded four separate analyses following the procedures outlined by the literature (Hair et al. 2009). The results of the multi-group comparison confirmed configural invariance (CFI 0.96; RMSEA 0.05) and factor loading equivalence (CFI 0.98; RMSEA 0.05; with an insignificant change in chi-square of 6.9/df 747). These values indicate metric invariance, which implies that the samples represented the same general population (Hair et al. 2009). Therefore, we proceeded with an analysis based on pooled data.

We incorporated a partial disaggregation approach (e.g., Sweeney et al. 1999) in order to investigate and confirm that all items of the EXQ dimensions truly represented the corresponding latent construct; this approach is widely used in scale-development studies (Dagger et al. 2007). The partial disaggregation approach is a compromise between an aggregate approach, in which all items are summed to form a single composite indicator of a construct, and a disaggregate approach, in which each item is treated as an individual indicator of the relevant factor (e.g., Bagozzi & Foxall 1996). Partial disaggregation overcomes the difficulties inherent in a disaggregate model by reducing random error and producing more stable estimates while maintaining the multiple indicator approach to structural equation modeling (e.g. Dabholkar et al. 1996). We operationalized the composite items applied to the partial disaggregation approach according to the guidelines set forth in the literature (e.g., Garver & Mentzer 1999). On this basis, items reflecting a particular construct were grouped at random to form a composite indicator. The assignment of items to composites is arbitrary as all items reflecting a latent construct are assumed to represent that construct in a similar fashion (Sweeney et al. 1999).

We assessed the fit of the measurement and structural models examined through multiple indices, as recommended by Hoyle and Panter (1995). It has been suggested that a chi-square value two or three times as large as the degrees of freedom is acceptable (Carmines & McIver 1981), but the fit is considered better the closer the chi-square value (CMIN) is to the degrees of freedom (df) for a model (Thacker et al. 1989). EXQ's CMIN/ df ratio displays an excellent fit. We used measures of incremental fit as indicators of acceptable model fit. In particular, we selected the type-2 incremental fit index (IFI), type-3 comparative fit index (CFI) and root mean square error of approximation (RMSEA). Type-2 IFI and type-3 CFI were selected based on their robustness to sample size variations (Hoyle & Panter 1995). We adopted the recommended threshold of >0.90 as indicative of adequate model fit for these indices (i.e. IFI, CFI). The accepted level for the RMSEA measure was <0.10, with lower values indicating better model fit (Hair et al. 2009, p. 772). Thus, EXQ's RMSEA score of 0.05 demonstrates an excellent model fit. The scale statistics indicate the robustness of the EXQ model (Hoyle & Panter 1995; Garver & Mentzer 1999) on the basis of the fit criteria established in prior service quality and CX research (e.g., Parasuraman et al. 2005).

Next, we evaluated the psychometric properties of the scale through a comprehensive CFA. We tested all items in the same model and restricted the items to load on their respective factors. The results are a sign of high levels of construct reliability and average variance extracted for all latent variables. All t values were significant ($p = 0.05$) and the average variances extracted were >0.50, and thus convergent validity was established. We established construct reliability with estimates exceeding 0.50, using

Fornell and Larcker's (1981) stringent criteria for measuring the internal consistency of a scale and its ability to measure a latent construct. Scale reliability was assessed using Fornell and Larcker's (1981) construct reliability formula: CREL = $(\Sigma\lambda)^2/[(\Sigma\lambda)^2 + \Sigma(1 - \lambda_j^2)]$. This formula measures the internal consistency of a scale and its ability to measure a latent construct. According to this approach, construct reliability estimates exceeding 0.50 are indicative of acceptable scale reliability (Fornell & Larcker 1981). After establishing the strength and psychometric properties of the scales underpinning the model, we examined the structure of the model. We modeled CX as suggested by researchers as a formative construct in which the dimensions of the model drive CX perceptions (Dagger et al., 2007). It is noteworthy that these scale items are specified as reflective based on the decision criteria of Jarvis, MacKenzie, and Podsakoff (2003). At the dimensional level, Jarvis et al. (2003) suggested that the formative approach is appropriate in the following circumstances: (a) when the direction of causality is from the dimensions to the construct, the dimensions serve as defining characteristics of the construct, and changes in the dimensions should cause changes in the construct; and (b) when the dimensions do not have the same or similar content, do not necessarily co-vary and do not have the same antecedents or consequences. On the basis of these criteria, we treated the dimensions as formative indicators of the higher order CX construct (see Figure 10.1). At the measurement level (item level), Jarvis et al. (2003) suggested that the reflective approach is appropriate when the following apply: (a) the relative homogeneity and interchangeability of scale items is high; (b) the degree of co-variation among items within each dimension is high; and (c) indicators within each dimension are likely to be affected by the same antecedents and have similar consequences. The relative homogeneity, and hence interchangeability, of scale items within each dimension, the high degree of co-variation among items within each dimension, and the expectation that indicators within each dimension (e.g., interpersonal skills) are likely to be affected by the same antecedents (e.g., branch) and therefore have similar consequences. In addition, we conducted second-order CFAs in which the dimensions of EXQ (e.g., *brand experience*) were modeled as reflective indicators of a second-order overall customer experience (EXQ) construct.

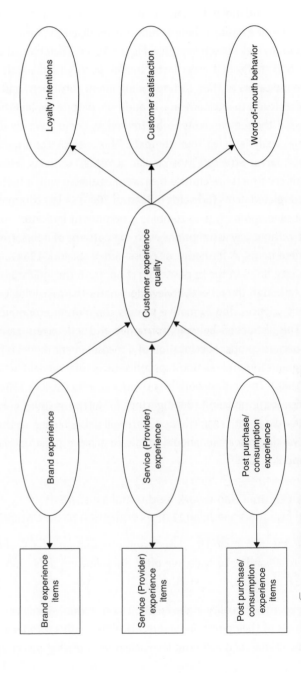

FIG 10.1 Conceptual model customer experience quality

The CFA analysis and model fit statistics were analogous to those reported in this study. On the basis of these criteria, we modeled the measurement aspect of our model reflectively (see Figure 10.1). Therefore, the CFA results reported are for first-order factor models specifying the scale items as reflective indicators of their corresponding latent constructs, and allow the latent constructs to intercorrelate. In addition, despite the fact that the data surpassed the requirements to be treated as pooled, we conducted an individual analysis of all four contexts. The analysis confirmed that the observed factor structure was similar across all contexts. However, not all latent constructs are entities that are measurable with a battery of positively correlated items (Edwards & Bagozzi 2000). A less common, but equally plausible approach is to combine a number of indicators to form a construct without any assumptions as to the patterns of intercorrelation between these items. A formative or causal index (Blalock 1964) results, where causality flows in the opposite direction, from the indicator to the construct. Although the reflective view dominates the psychological and management sciences, the formative view is common in economics and sociology. The distinction between formative and reflective measures is important because proper specification of a measurement model is necessary to assign meaningful relationships in the structural model (Anderson & Gerbing 1988). Theoretical work in construct validity (Blalock 1982) and structural equation modeling (Baumgartner & Homburg 1996) enhances our understanding, yet considerable debate still exists regarding the procedures a working researcher should follow to achieve construct validity (Diamantopoulos 2005).

Stage 4: Conceptual framework, additional assessment (Structural Equation Modelling) and connection to outcomes

Considering the above findings, our conceptualization of CX and the resulting reliable and valid scale, we offer the following definition of CX quality (see Figure 10.1):

Customer experience quality is the customer's dynamic value assessment of all attributes of their direct and indirect dealings with a company on an overall, dimensional, and attribute level, each level driving perception of the level above. Customer experience quality constitutes three dimensions, namely: brand experience, service (firm) experience and post-purchase/consumption experience. These evaluations of the customer experience drive important marketing outcomes, namely customer satisfaction, loyalty intentions, and word-of-mouth behavior.

To establish nomological validity, we examine how well the EXQ scale relates to other variables. Thus, in addition to the EXQ scale, the questionnaire included a five-item Behavioral Loyalty Scale (Parasuraman et al. 2005) based on a 13-item battery developed by Zeithaml et al. (1996), adapted a five-item Customer Satisfaction scale (Dagger et al. 2007), and incorporated a seven-item Word-of-Mouth Behaviors scale (Brown et al. 2005). These measures (see Appendix B) allowed us to capture the full range of potential behaviors likely to be triggered by CX (Mascarenhas et al. 2006). To demonstrate that a measure has nomological validity, the correlation between the measure and other related constructs should behave as expected in theory (Churchill 1995). In order to further demonstrate the discriminant validity of the EXQ scale, we compared the explanatory power of EXQ with the predominant measure of service quality, SERVQUAL (Parasuraman et al. 1988). We established this comparison by collecting data from survey respondents answering in alternating format first the EXQ and, normally 1–2 days later, the SERVQUAL questionnaire (or vice versa). We included only respondents answering both questionnaires in our data analysis. The samples used are the ones collected for the CFA described in stage 3. The SERVQUAL data was analyzed using an expectation minus perception difference score, as advocated by Parasuraman, Berry and Zeithaml (1993), measuring the overall impact of service quality on customer satisfaction, loyalty intentions, and word-of-mouth. We note that researchers frequently criticized SERVQUAL, and some might propose to use SERVPERF, a more complex model, to compare the perception of service quality and CX (Cronin & Taylor 1992). We decided to use SERVQUAL because, despite its critics, it is still the most widely used and referenced measure of service quality.

Scholars posit CX as a key determinant of customer satisfaction and loyalty (e.g., Caruana 2002; Schmitt 2003). Customer experience and customer satisfaction, while discrete constructs (Garbarino & Johnson 1999), are connected through a contributory relationship (Fornell 1992). Research submits that CX drives customer satisfaction, which in turn drives loyalty (e.g., Shankar et al. 2003). Marketing scholars acknowledge the link between customer satisfaction and loyalty intentions (Yi & La 2004). The exact nature of this relationship is still questioned because customer satisfaction is a desirable but not adequate condition for behavioral intentions (Koenig-Lewis & Palmer 2008). Therefore, this study explores the influence of CX on customer satisfaction and loyalty intentions independently. Researchers state that CX not only drives customer satisfaction (e.g., Anderson & Mittal 2000) and loyalty (McDougall & Levesque 2000; Fornell et al. 2006), but also word-of-mouth (Keiningham et al. 2007). The direct and indirect influences of CX on word-of-mouth are widely discussed in the literature in traditional offline (Babin et al. 2005), online (e.g., Hennig-Thurau et al. 2004), and experiential settings (e.g., Klaus & Maklan 2011). Subsequently, our study additionally explored the proposed relationship between customer experience and word-of-mouth behavior. We assessed scale reliability with a composite reliability coefficient (ranging from 0.92 to 0.97) and CFA, which clearly confirmed the appropriateness of the operationalizations (see Table 7.1).

As can be seen, our model fitted the data more than satisfactorily, signifying the substantial and positive relationships between EXQ and important marketing outcomes, namely customer satisfaction, loyalty, and word-of-mouth behavior. Examination of the structural parameters reveals that brand experience has a great effect on customer satisfaction and word-of-mouth behavior. Brand experience also displays a great effect on loyalty intentions. The service (firm) experience has the greatest effect of all three dimensions on customer satisfaction, a great effect on word-of-mouth behavior, and a high, but slightly lower, influence on loyalty intentions. Post-purchase/consumption experience displays by far the greatest effect of all dimensions on loyalty intentions and word-of-mouth behavior, and a great effect on customer satisfaction.

Service quality, measured by SERVQUAL, was found to significantly influence customer satisfaction (0.49), loyalty intentions (0.47), and word-of-mouth behavior (0.45). We propose, guided by our review of the literature, in which researchers advocate CX as the new and improved conceptualization and measurement of service quality, that CX quality will have a greater total effect on customers' intentions and behavior. When comparing the influence of both constructs on important marketing outcomes, CX was found to have a greater total effect on loyalty intentions, and a significant higher positive impact on customer satisfaction and word-of-mouth behavior than service quality (see Tables 7.2 and 7.3).

Discussion

Our study develops and validates a three-dimensional conceptualization of CX quality and the corresponding items for each dimension by the means of a scale-development process. We assessed the resulting scale EXQ through validity and reliability analysis of two scale-data collections, assuring the sufficient conceptualization of CX through the scale. We established nomological and discriminant validity of the scale by linking the scale dimensions and the overall scale to important marketing outcomes and comparing it with the well-established SERVQUAL scale.

EXQ can be employed as an analytical tool to detect poor and/or excellent CX performances across several functions within the company and/ or across various locations within the company across time. Another application of the scale is to benchmark within the company or a specific industry.

The findings suggest that customers base their perceptions of CX quality on three dimensions: *brand experience, service (firm) experience, and post-purchase/consumption experience.* The findings indicate that customers evaluate CX quality at an overall level, a dimensional level and an attribute level, and that each level drives perception on the level above. The research improves our understanding of how customers evaluate CX quality by linking their evaluation to important marketing outcomes, namely customer satisfaction, loyalty intentions, and word-of-mouth behavior.

Our findings confirm that all three dimensions of CX quality have a positive and significant impact on important marketing outcomes, validating the notion that the CX evaluation goes beyond the direct service encounter, and includes direct and indirect encounters with all functions of the company and possible channels and touch-points, such as marketing communications, advertising, internet presence and after-sales care (e.g., Payne et al. 2008; Voss et al. 2008). Investigating the influence of each individual dimension on the outcomes, the study depicts that the brand experience – the pre-encounter dimension – has an equally significant influence on all outcomes. The service (firm) experience has the most significant influence of all dimensions on customer satisfaction, confirming the suggested causal chain between the service encounter and customer satisfaction (e.g., Parasuraman et al. 1988). However, the dimension post-purchase/consumption has the greatest influence on both loyalty intentions and word-of-mouth behavior, confirming prior research (e.g., Maxham 2001). This dimension is highly relevant because of its close link to direct interactions and the resulting CXs with the service company. Based on their own first-hand experiences with the service company, customers have the ability to evaluate not only the companies' offerings, but also the experiences connected with these interactions. These findings suggest the importance of past experiences with the service company in forming positive behavioral intentions (Voss & Zomerdijk 2007) and influencing loyalty (e.g., Buttle & Burton 2002). The research confirms the notion that the means–end approach guiding the study serves to explain the differences between pre- and post-purchase evaluations in relation to marketing outcomes (Westbrook 1987).

Appendices

Appendix A

Sample profiles used in EFA

Variable	Professional service	Mass service	Service shop	Hedonic service
Age: Under 18	–	2.00	–	1.00
18–24	4.00	6.00	8.00	7.00
25–34	30.00	31.00	27.00	30.00
35–44	27.00	29.00	25.00	27.00
45–54	21.00	17.00	23.00	20.00
55–64	15.00	13.00	12.00	9.00
65+	3.00	3.00	5.00	6.00
Gender: Male	66.00	63.00	60.00	62.00
Female	34.00	37.00	40.00	38.00
Educational background: high school or less	30.00	30.00	34.00	30.00
Some college	48.00	36.00	40.00	34.00
College graduate	14.00	16.00	17.00	51.00
Graduate school	8.00	8.00	9.00	10.00
Annual household income: (growth in US$): up to $20000	3.00	4.00	3.00	4.00
$20001–$45000	20.00	21.00	18.00	16.00
$45001–$75000	20.00	25.00	22.00	18.00

(continued)

Continued

Variable	Professional service	Mass service	Service shop	Hedonic service
$75000–$125000	29.00	29.00	28.00	30.00
$125000–$250000	23.00	17.00	25.00	26.00
More than $250000	5.00	4.00	4.00	6.00

Note: Numbers did not sum to 100 in all instances, and are rounded to the next digit before .00 for expositional convenience.

Appendix B

Measures of study constructs – EXQ

Respondents rated their customer experience on each scale item using a 7-point scale (1 = strongly disagree, 7 = strongly agree) or as Do not know/Not applicable. The items below are grouped by dimensions for expositional convenience; they appeared in random order in the survey. The symbols preceding the items correspond to the variables named in Figure 10.1.

Brand experience
BRE1   XYZ has a good reputation.
BRE2   I am confident in XYZ's expertise.
BRE3   XYZ gives independent advice (on which product/service will best suit my needs).
BRE4   I choose XYZ not because of the price alone.
BRE5   The people who work at XYZ represent the XYZ brand well.
BRE6   XYZ's offerings have the best quality.
BRE7   XYZ's offerings are superior.

Service (firm) experience
SPE1   XYZ advised me throughout the process.
SPE2   Dealing with XYZ is easy.
SPE3   XYZ keeps me informed.
SPE4   XYZ demonstrates flexibility in dealing with me.
SPE5   At XYZ I always deal with the same forms and/or same people.
SPE6   XYZ's personnel relates to my wishes and concerns.
SPE7   The people I am dealing with (at XYZ) have good people skills.
SPE8   XYZ delivers a good customer service.
SPE9   I have built a personal relationship with the people at XYZ.
SPE10   XYZ's facilities are better designed to fulfill my needs than their competitors.

SPE11 XYZ's (online and/or offline) facilities are designed to be as efficient as possible (for me).

Post-purchase/consumption experience

PPE1 I stay with XYZ because they know me.
PPE2 XYZ knows exactly what I want.
PPE3 XYZ keeps me up-to-date.
PPE4 XYZ will look after me for a long time.
PPE5 XYZ deal(t) well with me when things go(went) wrong.
PPE6 I am happy with XYZ as my (service firm).
PPE7 Being a client at/customer of XYZ gives me social approval.

Behavioral loyalty intentions (Parasuraman et al. 2005; Zeithaml et al. 1996) Respondents rated their likelihood on each scale item using a 7-point scale (1 = not at all likely, 7 = extremely likely) or as Do not know/Not applicable. The items below were grouped as outlined below on the survey.

How likely are you to …

L1 Say positive things about XYZ to other people?
L2 Recommend XYZ to someone who seeks your advice?
L3 Encourage friends and relatives to use XYZ?
L4 Consider XYZ the first choice to buy – services?
L5 Use XYZ more in the next few years?

Customer satisfaction (e.g., Dagger et al. 2007) Respondents rated each item using a 7-point scale (1 = strongly disagree, 7 = strongly agree) or as Do not know/Not applicable.

SAT1 My feelings towards XYZ are very positive.
SAT2 I feel good about coming to XYZ for the offerings I am looking for.
SAT3 Overall I am satisfied with XYZ and the service they provide.
SAT4 I feel satisfied that XYZ produce the best results that can be achieved for me.
SAT5 The extent to which XYZ has produced the best possible outcome for me is satisfying.

Word-of-mouth behavior (Brown et al. 2005) Respondents rated "How much they did the following" on each scale item using a 7-point scale (1 = never, 7 = frequently) or as Do not know/Not applicable. The items below were grouped by dimensions as outlined below on the survey.

WOM1 Mentioned to others that you do business with XYZ.
WOM2 Made sure that others know that you do business with XYZ.
WOM3 Spoke positively about XYZ employee(s) to others.

WOM4   Recommended XYZ to family members.
WOM5   Spoke positively of XYZ to others.
WOM6   Recommended XYZ to acquaintances.
WOM7   Recommended XYZ to close personal friends.

SERVQUAL (Parasuraman et al. 1988, 1991)

This survey deals with your opinions of services. Please show the extent to which you think firms offering services should possess the features described by each statement. Do this by picking one of the seven numbers next to each statement. If you strongly agree that these firms should possess a feature, choose the number 7. If you strongly disagree that these firms should possess a feature, choose number 1. If your feelings are not strong, circle one of the numbers in the middle. There are no right or wrong answers – all we are interested in is a number that best shows your expectations about firms offering services.[1]

El. They should have up-to-date equipment.

E2. Their physical facilities should be visually appealing.

E3. Their employees should be well dressed and appear neat.

E4. The appearance of the physical facilities of these firms should be in keeping with the type of services provided.

E5. When these firms promise to do something by a certain time, they should do so.

E6. When customers have problems, these firms should be sympathetic and reassuring.

E7. These firms should be dependable.

E8. They should provide their services at the time they promise to do so.

E9. They should keep their records accurately.

E10. They shouldn't be expected to tell customers exactly when services will be performed.[2]

Ell. It is not realistic for customers to expect prompt service from employees of these firms. (–)

E12. Their employees don't always have to be willing to help customers. (–)

El3. It is okay if they are too busy to respond to customer requests promptly. (–)

E14. Customers should be able to trust employees of these firms.

El5. Customers should be able to feel safe in their transactions with these firms' employees.

El6. Their employees should be polite.

E17. Their employees should get adequate support from these firms to do their jobs well.

El8. These firms should not be expected to give customers individual attention. (-)

E19. Employees of these firms cannot be expected to give customers personal attention. (–)

E20. It is unrealistic to expect employees to know what the needs of their customers are. (–)

E21. It is unrealistic to expect these firms to have their customers' best interests at heart. (–)

E22. They shouldn't be expected to have operating hours convenient to all their customers. (–)

The following set of statements relates to your feelings about XYZ. For each statement, please show the extent to which you believe XYZ has the feature described by the statement. Once again, marking a 1 means that you strongly disagree that XYZ has that feature, and marking a 7 means that you strongly agree. You may circle any of the numbers in the middle that show how strong your feelings are. There are no right or wrong answers – all we are interested in is a number that best shows your perceptions about XYZ.

Pl. XYZ has up-to-date equipment.

P2. XYZ's physical facilities are visually appealing.

P3. XYZ's employees are well dressed and appear neat.

P4. The appearance of the physical facilities of XYZ is in keeping with the type of services provided.

P5. When XYZ promises to do something by a certain time, it does so.

P6. When you have problems, XYZ is sympathetic and reassuring.

P7. XYZ is dependable.

P8. XYZ provides its services at the time it promises to do so.

P9. XYZ keeps its records accurately.

P10. XYZ does not tell customers exactly when services will be performed. (–)

P11. You do not receive prompt service from XYZ's employees. (–)

P12. Employees of XYZ are not always willing to help customers. (–)

P13. Employees of XYZ are too busy to respond to customer requests promptly. (–)

P14. You can trust employees of XYZ.

P15. You feel safe in your transactions with XYZ's employees.

P16. Employees of XYZ are polite.

P17. Employees get adequate support from XYZ to do their jobs well.

P18. XYZ does not give you individual attention. (–)

P19. Employees of XYZ do not give you personal attention. (–)

P20. Employees of XYZ do not know what your needs are. (–)

P21. XYZ does not have your best interests at heart. (–)

P22. XYZ does not have operating hours convenient to all their customers. (–)

Typology data analysis details

The questionnaire comprised a scale with 48 items and various business and personal demographic and behavioral questions. Data was analysed using the SPSS and Latent Gold software packages. SPSS was used to conduct univariate analysis followed by multivariate analysis in the form of factor analysis. Given that the data for the latter analysis violated various assumptions necessary for parametric multivariate analysis, an alternative latent class modeling technique that does not require such stringent characteristics was employed using the Latent Gold software. The results of the univariate analysis were presented first, followed by the Latent Gold latent class technique, and then the factor analysis results were performed using SPSS.

Notes

Appendices

1. A seven-point scale ranging from "Strongly disagree" (1) to "Strongly agree" (7), with no verbal labels for the intermediate scale points (i.e., 2 through 6), accompanies each statement. Also, the statements are in random order in the questionnaire.
2. (–) stands for items scored in reverse order.

References

Abbott, Lawrence (1955), *Quality and Competition: An Essay in Economic Theory,* New York: Columbia University Press.

Adelman, Leonard and Terry Bresnick (1992), "Examining the Effect of Information Sequence on Patriot Air Defence Officer Judgements," *Organizational Behaviour and Human Decision Processes*, 53 (November), 204–228.

Ajzen, Icek and Martin Fishbein (1977), "Attitude-Behavior Relations: A Theoretical Analysis and Review of Empirical Research," *Psychological Bulletin*, 84 (5), 888–918.

Alderson, Wroe (1957), *Marketing Behaviour and Executive Education,* Homewood, IL: Irwin.

Anderson, Eugene W. and Vikas Mittal (2000), "Strengthening the Satisfaction-profit Chain," *Journal of Service Research*, 3 (2), 107–120.

Anderson, Eugene W., Caes Fornell, and Donald R. Lehmann (1994), "Customer Satisfaction, Market Share, and Profitability: Findings from Sweden," *Journal of Marketing*, 58 (3), 53–66.

Anderson, James C. and David W. Gerbing (1988), "Structural Equation Modeling in Practice: A Review and Recommended Two-step Approach," *Psychological Bulletin*, 103 (3), 411–423.

Armstrong, J. Scott and Terry S. Overton (1977), "Estimating Nonresponse Bias in Mail Surveys," *Journal of Marketing Research,* 14 (August), 396–402.

Arnould, Eric J. and Price, Linda L. (1993), "River Magic: Extraordinary Experience and the Extended Service Encounter," *Journal of Consumer Research*, 20 (1), 24–45.

Arussy, Lior (2002), "Don't Take Calls, Make Contact," *Harvard Business Review*, 80 (1), 16–18.

Auzair, Sofiah Md. and Kim Langfield-Smith (2005), "The Effect of Service Process Type, Business Strategy and Life Cycle Stage on Bureaucratic MCS in Service Companies," *Management Accounting Research*, 16 (4), 399–421.

Babin, Barry J., Yong-Ki Lee, Eun-Ju Kim, and Mitch Griffin (2005), "Modeling Consumer Satisfaction and Word-of-mouth: Restaurant Patronage in Korea," *Journal of Services Marketing*, 19 (3), 133–139.

Badgett, Melody, Mauren Stancik S. Moyce, and Herb Kleinberger (2007), *Turning Shoppers into Advocates*. IBM Institute for Business Value.

Bagozzi, Richard P. (2000), "On the Concept of Intentional Social Action in Consumer Behavior," *Journal of Consumer Research*, 27 (3), 388–396.

Bagozzi, Richard P. and Gordon R. Foxall (1996), "Construct Validation of a Measure of Adaptive-Innovative Cognitive Styles in Consumption," *International Journal of Research in Marketing*, 13 (3), 201–213.

Bagozzi, Richard P. and Todd F. Heatherton (1994), "A General Approach to Representing Multifaceted Personality Constructs: Application to State Self-esteem," *Structural Equation Modeling*, 1 (1), 35–67.

Baker, Julie, A. Parasuraman, Dhruv Grewal, and Glenn B. Voss (2002), "The Influence of Multiple Store Environment Cues on Perceived Merchandise Value and Patronage Intentions," *Journal of Marketing*, 66 (2), 120–141.

Ballantyne, David and Richard J. Varey (2006), "Creating Value-in-use through Marketing Interaction: The Exchange Logic of Relating, Communicating and Knowing," *Marketing Theory*, 6 (3), 335–348.

Bansal, Harvir S., Gordon H.G. McDougall, Shane S. Dikolli, and Karen L. Sedatole (2004), "Relating e-satisfaction to Behavioral Outcomes: An Empirical Study," *Journal of Services Marketing*, 18 (4), 290–302.

Beldad, A., De Jong, M., and Steehouder, M. (2010), "How shall I trust the faceless and the intangible? A literature review on the antecedents of online trust," *Computers in Human Behavior*, 26 (5), 857–869.

Belk, Russell W., Melanie Wallendorf, and John F. Sherry, Jr. (1989), "The Sacred and the Profane in Consumer Behavior: Theodicy on the Odyssey," *The Journal of Consumer Research*, 16 (1), 1–38.

Berry, Leonard L., Lewis P. Carbone and Stephan H. Haeckel (2002), "Managing the Total Customer Experience," *MIT Sloan Management Review*, 43 (3), 85–89.

Berry, Leonard L., Eileen A. Wall, and Lewis P. Carbone (2006), "Service Clues and Customer Assessment of the Service Experience: Lessons from Marketing," *Academy of Management Perspectives*, 20 (2), 43–57.

Bitner, Mary Jo (1992), "Servicescapes: The Impact of Physical Surroundings on Customers and Employees," *Journal of Marketing*, 56 (April), 57–71.

Blumler, Jay G. (1979), "The Role of Theory in Uses and Gratifications Studies," *Communication Research*, 6 (2), 9–33.

Bolton, Ruth N. and James H. Drew (1991), "A Longitudinal Analysis of the Impact of Service Changes on Customer Attitudes," *Journal of Marketing*, 55 (January), 1–9.

Bolton, Ruth N. (1998), "A dynamic model of the duration of the customer's relationship with a continuous service provider: the role of satisfaction," *Marketing science*, 17 (1), 45–65.

Botschen, Günther, Eva M. Thelen, and Rik Pieters (1999), "Using Means-end Structures for Benefit Segmentation: An Application to Services," *European Journal of Marketing*, 33 (1), 38–58.

Boulding, W., Kalra, A., Staelin, R., and Zelthaml, V. A. (1993), "A Dynamic Process Model of Service Quality: From Expectations to Behavioral Intentions," *Journal of Marketing Research*.

Bowman, D. and Narayandas, D. (2004), "Linking Customer Management Effort to Customer Profitability in Business Markets," *Journal of Marketing Research (JMR)*, 41 (4), 433–447.

Boyer, Kenneth K. and G. Thomas M. Hult (2006), "Customer Behavioral Intentions for Online Purchases: An Examination of Fulfillment Method and Customer Experience Level," *Journal of Operations Management,* 24 (2), 124–147.

Brady, Michael K. and J. Joseph Cronin (2001), "Customer Orientation – Effects on Customer Service Perceptions and Outcome Behaviors," *Journal of Service Research*, 3 (3), 241–251.

Brakus, J. Josko, Bernd H. Schmitt, and Lia Zarantonello (2009), "Brand Experience: What is It? How is It Measured? Does it Affect Loyalty?," *Journal of Marketing*, 73 (3), 52–68.

Brocato, Deanne E., Clay M. Voorhees, and Julie Baker (2012), "Understanding the Influence of Cues from Other Customers in the Service Experience: A Scale Development and Validation," *Journal of Retailing*, 88 (3), 384–398.

Brodie, Roderick J., Mark S. Glynn, and Victoria Little (2006), "The Service Brand and the Service-dominant Logic: Missing Fundamental Premise or the Need for Stronger Theory?" *Marketing Theory*, 6 (3), 363–379.

Brown, J., H. Manning, A. Stone, and C. O'Connor (2013), *Tools for Mastering the Customer Experience Ecosystem: Forrester*.

Brown, Tom J., Thomas E. Barry, Peter A. Dacin, and Richard F. Gunst (2005), "Spreading the Word: Investigating the Antecedents of Consumers' Positive Word-of-mouth Intentions and Behaviors in a Retailing Context," *Journal of the Academy of Marketing Science,* 33 (2), 123–138.

Burns, M. (2011). *The State of Customer Experience*. Forrester.

Burton, Suzan, Simon J. Sheather and John H. Roberts (2003), "Reality or Perception? The Effect of Actual and Perceived Performance on Satisfaction and Behavioral Intention," *Journal of Service Research*, 5 (4), 292–302.

Butler, Clay (1991), "The Waiting Game," *Successful Meetings*, 40 (3), 114–116.

Buttle, Francis (1996), "SERVQUAL: Review, Critique, Research Agenda," *European Journal of Marketing*, 30 (1), 8–32.

Buttle, Francis and Jamie Burton (2002), "Does Service Failure Influence Customer Loyalty?" *Journal of Consumer Behavior*, 1 (3), 217–227.

Carbone, Lewis P. (2004), *Clued in: How to Keep Customers Coming Back Again and Again*. Harlow, UK: FT Prentice Hall.

Carmines, Edward G. and John P. McIver (1981), "Analyzing Models with Unobserved Variables: Analysis of Covariance Structures," in G. Bohmstedt and E. Borgatta (eds), *Social Measurement: Current Issues*, Beverly Hills, CA: SAGE, pp. 65–115.

Carù, Atonella and Bernard Cova (2003), "Revisiting Consumption Experience. A More Humble but Complete View of the Concept," *Marketing Theory*, 3 (2), 267–286.

Caruana, Albert (2002), "Service Loyalty: The Effects of Service Quality and the Mediating Role of Customer Satisfaction," *European Journal of Marketing*, 36 (7/8), 811–829.

Castellanos, T., M. Hernandez-Kakol and D. Huang (2011), Seven steps to better customer experience management – Improving customer management to drive profitable growth: KPMG.

Christensen, Clayton M., Scott Cook, and Taddy Hall (2005), "Marketing Malpractice: The Cause and the Cure," *Harvard Business Review*, 83 (12), 74–83.

Churchill, Gilbert A. Jr. (1979), "A Paradigm for Developing Better Measures of Marketing Constructs," *Journal of Marketing Research*, 16 (1), 64–73.

Churchill, Gilbert A. Jr. (1995), *Marketing Research Methodological Foundations*, 6th edition, Dryden Press, Fort Worth, TX.

Clisbee, Mary (2003), "Using N-vivo for Literature Analysis: Strategies in Qualitative Research: Methodological Issues and Practices Using QSR NVivo and NUD*IST," University of London, London, UK.

Cova, Bernard (1996), "What Postmodernism Means to Marketing Managers," *European Management Journal*, 14 (5), 494–499.

Coviello, Nicole E., Roderick J. Brodie, Peter J. Danaher and Wesley J. Johnston (2002), "How Firms Relate to Their Markets: An Empirical Examination of Contemporary Marketing Practices," *Journal of Marketing*, 66 (3), 33–46.

Cowley, Elizabeth (2008), "Looking Back at an Experience Through Rose-colored Glasses," *Journal of Business Research*, 61 (10), 1046–1052.

Cronin, J. Joseph Jr. and Steven A. Taylor (1992), "Measuring Service Quality: A Reexamination and Extension," *Journal of Marketing*, 56 (7), 55–68.

Csikszentmihalyi, Mihaly (1988), "The Flow Experience and Human Psychology," in M. Csikszentmihalyi and I. S. Csikszentmihalyi (eds), *Optimal Experience: Psychological Studies of Flow in Consciousness*, New York: Cambridge University Press, pp. 15–35.

Dabholkar, Pratibha A. and Richard P. Bagozzi (2002), "An Attitudinal Model of Technology Based Self-Service: Moderating Effects of Consumer Traits and Situational Factors," *Journal of Academy of Marketing Science,* 30 (3), 184–201.

Dabholkar, Pratibha A., Dayle I. Thorpe, and Joseph O. Rentz (1996), "A Measure of Service Quality for Retail Stores: Scale Development and Validation," *Journal of the Academy of Marketing Science,* 24 (1), 3–16.

Dagger, et al. (2007), "A Hierarchical Model of Health Service Quality: Scale-development and Investigation of an Integrated Model," *Journal of Service Research,* 10 (2), 123–142.

Dewey, John (1963), *Experience and Education,* Collier, New York, NY.

Di Gregorio, Silvana (2000), "Using Nvivo for Your Literature Review," paper presented at conference on Strategies in Qualitative Research: Issues and Results from Analysis using QSR Nvivo and NUD*IST, 29–30 September, Institute of Education, London, available at: http://www.sdgassociates.com/downloads/literature_review.pdf (accessed 3 August 2011).

Diamantopoulos, Adamantios (2005), "The C-OAR-SE Procedure for Scale Development in Marketing: A Comment," *International Journal of Research in Marketing,* 22 (1), 1–9.

Diamantopoulos, Adamantios and Heidi M. Winklhofer (2001), "Index Construction with Formative Indicators: An Alternative to Scale Development," *Journal of Marketing Research,* 38 (2), 269–277.

Dick, Alan S. and Kunal Basu (1994), "Customer Loyalty: Toward an Integrated Conceptual Framework," *Journal of the Academy of Marketing Science,* 22 (2), 99–113.

Doty, Harold, D. and Glick, William, H (1994), "Typologies As a Unique Form Of Theory Building: Toward Improved Understanding and Modeling," *Academy of Management Review,* 9 (2), 230–251.

Dreyfus, Hubert L. and Stuart E. Dreyfus (1986), *Mind over Machine,* New York: The Free Press.

Edvardsson, Bo and Inger Roos (2001), "Critical Incident Techniques: Towards a Framework for Analysing the Criticality of Critical Incidents," *International Journal of Service Industry Management,* 12 (3), 251–268.

Edvardsson, Bo and Tore Strandvik (2000), "Is a Critical Incident Critical for a Customer Relationship?" *Managing Service Quality,* 10 (2), 82–91.

Edvardsson, Bo, Anders Gustafsson, and Inger Roos (2005), "Service Portraits in Service Research – a Critical Review," *International Journal of Service Industry Management,* 16 (1), 107–121.

Edvardsson, Bo, Bo Enquist, and Robert Johnston (2005), "Cocreating Customer Value through Hyperreality in the Prepurchase Service Experience," *Journal of Service Research,* 8 (2), 149–161.

Edvardsson, Bo, Bo Enquist, and Robert Johnston (2010), "Design Dimensions of Experience Rooms for Service Test Drives: Case studies in Several Service Contexts," *Managing Service Quality,* 20 (4), 312–327.

Edvardsson, Bo, Bård Tronvoll, and Thorsten Gruber (2011), "Expanding Understanding of Service Exchange and Value Co-creation: A Social Construction Approach," *Journal of the Academy of Marketing Science*, 39 (April), 327–339.

Eisenhardt, Kathleen M. (1998), "Better Stories and Better Constructs: The Case of Rigor nd Comparatice Logic," *Academy of Management Review*, 16 (3) 620–627.

Ericsson, K. Anders and Robert J. Crutcher (1990) "The Nature of Exceptional Performance," in P. B. Baltes, D. L. Featherman, and R. M. Lerner (eds), *Life-Span Development and Behavior*, vol. 10, Hillsdale, NJ: Erlbaum, pp. 187–218.

Finne, S., Girouard, B., and Jacobs, K. (2012), *All-Channel Experience: Digital Product Data*: Capgemini.

Firat, A. Fuat, Nikhilesh Dholakia, and Richard P. Bagozzi (1987), "Introduction: Breaking the Mold," in A. F. Firat, N. Dholakia, and R. P. Bagozzi (eds), *Philosophical and Radical Thought in Marketing*, Lexington, ID: Lexington Books, pp. 120–160.

Fitzsimons, Grainne M., Tanya L. Chartrand, and Gavan J. Fitzsimons (2008), "Automatic Effects of Brand Exposure on Motivated Behavior: How Apple Makes You 'Think Different'," *Journal of Consumer Research*, 35 (1), 21–35.

Ford, Robert C., Bo Edvardsson, Duncan Dickson, and Bo Enquist (2012), "Managing the Innovation Co-creation Challenge: Lesson from Service Exemplars Disney and IKEA," *Organizational Dynamics*, 41 (3), 281–290.

Forgas, Joseph P. (2000), *Feeling and Thinking: Affective Influences on Social Cognition*, New York: Cambridge University Press.

Fornell, Claes (1992), "A National Customer Satisfaction Barometer: The Swedish Experience," *Journal of Marketing*, 56 (1), 6–21.

Fornell, Claes and David F. Larcker (1981), "Evaluating Structural Equation Models with Unobservable Variables and Measurement Error," *Journal of Marketing Research*, 18 (1), 39–50.

Fornell, Claes, Sunil Mithas, Forrest V. Morgeson III, and M.S. Krishnan (2006), "Customer Satisfaction and Stock Prices: High Returns, Low Risk," *Journal of Marketing*, 70 (1), 3–14.

Frow, Pennie and Payne, Adrian (2007), "Towards the 'Perfect' Customer Experience," *Journal of Brand Management*, 15 (2), 89–101.

Funder, David C., Michael Furr, and Randal Colvin (2000), "The Riverside Behavioral Q-sort: A Tool for the Description of Social Behavior," *Journal of Personality*, 68 (3), 451–489.

Garbarino, Ellen and Mark S. Johnson (1999), "The Different Roles of Satisfaction, Trust, and Commitment in Customer Relationships," *Journal of Marketing*, 63 (2), 70–87.

Garfinkel, Harold (1967), *Studies in Ethnomethodology*, Englewood Cliffs, NJ: Prentice Hall.

Garver, Michael S. and John T. Mentzer (1999), "Logistics Research Methods: Employing Structural Equation Modeling to Test for Construct Validity," *Journal of Business Logistics*, 20 (1), 33–57.

Gentile, Chiara, Nicola Spiller, and Giuliano Noci (2007), "How to Sustain the Customer Experience: An Overview of Experience Components that Co-create Value With the Customer," *European Management Journal*, 25 (5), 395–410.

Girouard, B., Jacobs, K., and Helders, B. (2012), *All-Channel Experience: Engaging with Technology-Enabled Shoppers,* Capgemini.

Glaser, Barney G. (2002), "Conceptualization: On Theory and Theorizing using Grounded Theory," *International Journal of Qualitative Methods*, 1 (2), 1–31.

Glaser, Barney G. and Anselm L. Strauss (1967), *The Discovery of Grounded Theory: Strategies for Qualitative Research,* Chicago: Aldine Publishing Company.

Golder, Peter, N., Debanjan Mitra, and Christine Moorman (2012), "What is Quality? An Integrative Framework of Processes and States," *Journal of Marketing*, 76 (July), 1–23.

Goodwin, Cathy, Stephen J. Grove, and Raymond P. Fisk (1996), "Collaring the Cheshire Cat: Studying Customers' Service Experience through Metaphor," *The Service Industries Journal*, 16 (4), 421–442.

Grace, Debra and Aron O'Cass (2004), "Examining the Effects of Service Brand Communications on Brand Evaluation," *Journal of Product and Brand Management*, 14 (2), 106–116.

Gremler, Dwayne D. and Kevin P. Gwinner (2008), "Rapport-Building Behaviors Used by Retail Employees," *Journal of Retailing,* 84 (3), 308–324.

Grewal, Dhruv, Michael Levy, and V. Kumar (2009), "Customer Experience Management in Retailing: An Organizing Framework," *Journal of Retailing*, 85 (1), 1–14.

Gronroos, Christian (1997), "Value-driven Relational Marketing: From Products to Resources and Competencies," *Journal of Marketing Management*, 13 (5), 407–419.

Gruen, Thomas W., Talai Osmonbekov, and Andrew J. Czaplewski (2006), "eWOM: The Impact of Customer-to-customer Online Know-How Exchange on Customer Value and Loyalty," *Journal of Business Research*, 59 (4), 449–456.

Grunert, Klaus G. and Suzanne C. Grunert (1995), "Measuring Subjective Meaning Structures by the Laddering Method: Theoretical Considerations and Methodological Problems," *International Journal of Research in Marketing*, 12 (3), 209–225.

Guenzi, Paolo and Laurent Georges (2010), "Interpersonal Trust in Commercial Relationships: Antecedents and Consequences of Customer Trust in the Salesperson," *European Journal of Marketing*, 44 (1/2), 114–138.

Guest, Greg, Arwen Bunce, and Laura Johnson (2006), "How Many Interviews Are Enough? An Experiment with Data Saturation and Variability," *Field Methods*, 18(1), 59–82.

Haas, J. Eugene, Richard H. Hall, and Norman J. Johnson (1966), "Toward an Empirically Derived Taxonomy of Organizations," in R. V. Bowers (ed.), *Studies on Behavior in Organizations*, Athens, GA: University of Georgia Press, pp. 157–180.

Haeckel, Stephan H., Lewis P. Carbone and Leonard L. Berry (2003), "How to Lead the Customer Experience," *Marketing Management*, 12 (1), 18–23.

Hagen, P. (2013), *7 Ways to Engage Third-Party Providers for a Unified Customer Experience*, Forrester.

Hair, Joseph F., William Black, Barry Babin, and Rolph E. Anderson (2009), *Multivariate Data Analysis*, 7th edition, Upper Saddle River, NJ: Prentice Hall.

Hambrick, Donald C. (1984), "Taxonomic Approaches to Studying Strategy: Some Conceptual and Methodological Issues," *Journal of Management*, 10 (1), 27–41.

Hanssens, D. M., Rust, R. T., and Srivastava, R. K. (2009), "Marketing strategy and Wall Street: nailing down marketing's impact," *Journal of Marketing*, 73 (6), 115–118.

Hennig-Thurau, Thorsten, Kevin P. Gwinner, Gianfranco Walsh, and Dwayne D. Gremler (2004), "Electronic Word-of-mouth Via Consumer-opinion platforms: What Motivates Consumers to Articulate Themselves on the Internet?" *Journal of Interactive Marketing*, 18 (1), 38–52.

Heskett, James L., W. Earl Sasser, Jr., and Leonard A. Schlesinger. (1997), *The Service Profit Chain*, New York: Free Press.

Heskett, James L., W. Earl Sasser, Jr., and Leonard A. Schlesinger. (1997), *Service profit chain*. Simon and Schuster.

Hirschman, Elizabeth C. and Morris B. Holbrook (1982), "Hedonic Consumption: Emerging Concepts, Methods and Propositions," *Journal of Marketing*, 46 (3), 92–101.

Hoch, Stephen J. (2002), "Product Experience is Seductive," *Journal of Consumer Research*, 29 (3), 448–454.

Holbrook, Morris B. (1999), "Introduction to Consumer Value," in M. B. Holbrook (ed.), *Consumer Value: A Framework for Analysis and Research*, London: Routledge, pp. 1–28.

Holbrook, Morris B. (2006), "Book Reviews – The Consumption Experience," *Journal of Macromarketing*, 26 (2), 259–266.

Holbrook, Morris B. (2006), "Reply to Bradshaw, McDonagh, and Marshall: Turn off the Bubble Machine," *Journal of Macromarketing*, 26 (1), 84–88.

Hollander, D., Hertz, K., and Wassink, B. H. (2013), *The Journey Toward Greater Customer Centricity*. Ernst&Young.

Hora, Stephen C. and Detlov Von Winterfeldt (1997), "Natural Waste and Future Societies: A Deep Look into the Future," *Technological Forecasting and Social Change*, 56 (2), 155–170.

Howard, John A. and Jagdish N. Sheth (1969), *The Theory of Buyer Behavior*, New York, NY: John Wiley.

Hoyle, Rick H. and Abigail T. Panter (1995), "Writing About Structural Equation Models," in R. Hoyle (ed.), *Structural Equation Modeling*, Thousand Oaks, CA: SAGE, pp. 158–176.

Hudson, Darren, Lee-Hong Seah, Diane Hite, and Tim Haab (2004), "Telephone Presurveys, Self-selection, and Non-response Bias to Mail and Internet surveys in Economic Research," *Applied Economic Letters*, 11, 237–240.

Hult, G. Thomas M., David J. Ketchen, and Stanley F. Slater (2002), "A Longitudinal Study of the Learning Climate and Cycle Time in Supply Chains," *Journal of Business and Industrial Marketing*, 17 (4), 302–323.

Hume, Margee, Gillian Sullivan Mort, Peter W. Liesch, and Hume Winzar (2006), "Understanding Service Experience in Non-profit Performing Arts: Implications for Operations and Service Management," *Journal of Operations Management*, 24 (4), 304–324.

Hussain, Mostaq M. and Gin Chong (2008), "Non-financial Performance Measurement Practices in Financial Services Industry: An Agency Theory Approach," paper presented at CAAA annual conference, 11 January 2008, Winnipeg, Canada, available at http://ssrn.com/abstract=1082906.

Jarvis, Cheryl B., Scott B. MacKenzie, and Philip M. Podsakoff (2003), "A Critical Review of Construct Indicators and Measurement Model Misspecification in Marketing and Consumer Research," *Journal of Consumer Research*, 30 (2), 199–218.

Johnston, Wesley J. and Thomas V. Bonoma (1981), "The Buying Center: Structure and Interaction Patterns," *Journal of Marketing*, 45 (3), 143–156.

Johnston, Robert and Graham Clark (2008), *Service Operations Management*, 3rd edition, Financial Times/Prentice Hall, Pearson Education.

Jones, Peter (ed.) (2008), *Handbook of Hospitality Operations and IT* (Handbooks of Hospitality Management, Volume 1), Oxford: Butterworth-Heinemann.

Keiningham, Timothy L., Bruce Cooil, Lerzan Aksoy, Tor W. Andreassen, and Jay Weiner (2007), "The Value of Different Customer Satisfaction and Loyalty Metrics in Predicting Customer Retention, Recommendation and Share-of-wallet," *Managing Service Quality*, 17 (4), 361–384.

Keiningham, T. L., Aksoy, L., Malthouse, E. C., Lariviere, B., and Buoye, A. (2014), "The cumulative effect of satisfaction with discrete transactions on share of wallet," *Journal of Service Management*, 25 (3), 310–333.

Kelley, Scott W. and Mark A. Davis (1994), "Antecedents to Customer Expectations for Service Recovery," *Journal of the Academy of Marketing Science*, 22 (1), 52–61.

Keynes, John Maynard (1936), *The General Theory of Employment, Interest and Money*, Cambridge University Press, Cambridge.

Kim, A. J., and Ko, E. (2012), "Do social media marketing activities enhance customer equity? An empirical study of luxury fashion brand," *Journal of Business Research*, 65 (10), 1480–1486.

Klaus, Philipp (2011), "Quo Vadis, Customer Experience?" in C. Rusconi (ed.), *Beyond CRM: Customer Experience in the Digital Era. Strategies, Best Practices and Future Scenarios in Luxury and Fashion*, Milano: Franco Angeli, pp. 165–175.

Klaus, Philipp (2013), "The Case of Amazon.com: Towards a Conceptual Framework of Online Customer Service Experience (OCSE) Using Emerging Consensus Technique (ECT)," *Journal of Service Marketing*, 27 (6), 443–457.

Klaus, Philipp (2014), "Getting It Done – Delivering Superior Firm Performance through Holistic Customer Experience (CX) Strategies," in J. Kandampully (ed.), *Customer Experience Management: Enhancing Experience and Value through Service Management*, Dubuque, IA: Kendall Hunt.

Klaus, Philipp (2014), "Are You Providing the Right Luxury Experience? A Critical Examination of the After-Sales Services' Role on Customer Behaviour," in F. Courvoisier (ed.), *After Sales Services: New Demands*, Neuchatel, CH: Journées de Recherche en Marketing Horloger.

Klaus, Philipp (2014), "Towards Practical Relevance – Delivering Superior Firm Performance Through Digital Customer Experience Strategies," *Journal of Direct, Data, and Digital Marketing Practice*, 15, (4), 306–316.

Klaus, Philipp and Edvardsson, B. (2014), "Striking the right balance: How to design, implement, and operationalize Customer Experience Management programs," in Baglieri, E. and Karmarkar, U. (eds.), *Managing consumer services: Factory or Theatre?*, Springer, Berlin, pp. 69–90.

Klaus, Philipp and Stan Maklan (2007), "The Role of Brands in a Service Dominated World," *Journal of Brand Management*, 15 (2), 115–122.

Klaus, Philipp and Stan Maklan (2011), "Bridging the Gap for Destination Extreme Sports – A Model of Sports Tourism Customer Experience," *Journal of Marketing Management*, 27 (13–14), 1341–1365.

Klaus, Philipp and Stan Maklan (2012), "EXQ: A Multiple-item Scale for Assessing Service Experience," *Journal of Service Management*, 23 (1), 5–33.

Klaus, Philipp and Stan Maklan (2013), "Towards a Better Measure of Customer Experience," *International Journal of Market Research*, 55 (2), 227–246.

Klaus, Philipp, Edvardsson, Bo, and Stan Maklan, (2012), "Developing a Typology of Customer Experience Management Practice – From Preservers to Vanguards," 12th International Research Conference in Service Management, La Londe les Maures, France, May/June 2012.

Klaus, Philipp, Keiningham, Tim, Edvardsson, Bo, and Gruber, Thorsten (2014), "Getting in with the 'In' Crowd: How to Put Marketing Back on the CEO's Agenda," *Journal of Service Management*, 25 (2), 195–212.

Klaus, Philipp, Michele Gorgoglione, Umberto Pannelio, Daniela Buonamassa, and Bang Nguyen (2013), "Are You Providing the 'Right' Experiences? The Case of Banca Popolare di Bari," *International Journal of Bank Marketing*, 31 (7), 506–528.

Koenig-Lewis, Nicole and Palmer, Adrian (2008), "Experiential Values Over Time – a Comparison of Measures of Satisfaction and Emotion," *Journal of Marketing Management*, 24 (1–2), 69–85.

LaSalle, Diana and Terry Britton (2003), *Priceless: Turning Ordinary Products into Extraordinary Experiences*, Boston, MA: Harvard Business School Press.

Lebergott, Stanley (1993), *Pursuing Happiness: American Consumers in the Twentieth Century*, Princeton, NJ: Princeton University Press.

Lee, Gwo-Guang and Hsiu-Fen Lin (2005), "Customer Perceptions of e-service Quality in Online Shopping," *International Journal of Retail and Distribution Management*, 33 (2/3), 161–176.

Lemke, Fred, Moira Clark, and Hugh Wilson (2011), "Customer Experience Quality: An Exploration in Business and Consumer Contexts using Repertory Grid Technique," *Journal of the Academy of Marketing Science*, 39 (6), 846–869.

Luo, Xueming (2005), "How Does Shopping With Other Influence Impulsive Purchasing?" *Journal of Consumer Psychology*, 15 (4), 288–294.

Magidson, Jay and Vermunt, Jeroen K. (2005), *A Nontechnical Introduction to Latent Class Models*, Statistical Innovations, http://www.statisticalinnovations.com/articles/lcmodels2.pdf.

Maklan, Stan and Philipp Klaus (2011), "Customer Experience: Are We Measuring the Right Things", *International Journal of Market Research*, 53 (6), 771–792.

Mantrala, Murali K., Michael Levy, Barbara E. Kahn, Edward J. Fox, Peter Gaidarev, Bill Dankworth, and Denish Shah (2009), "Why is Assortment Planning so Difficult for Retailers? A Framework and Research Agenda," *Journal of Retailing*, 85 (1), 71–83.

Mascarenhas, Oswald A., Ram Kesavan, and Michael Bernacchi (2006), "Lasting Customer Loyalty: A Total Customer Experience Approach," *Journal of Consumer Marketing*, 23 (7), 397–405.

Mattila, Anna S. and Cathy A. Enz (2002), "The Role of Emotions in Service Encounters," *Journal of Service Research*, 4 (4), 268–277.

Maxham, James G. III. (2001), "Service Recovery's Influence on Consumer Satisfaction, Positive Word-of-Mouth and Purchase Intentions," *Journal of Business Research*, 54 (1), 11–24.

McColl-Kennedy, Janet R., Paul G. Patterson, Amy K. Smith, and Michael K. Brady (2009), "Customer Rage Episodes: Emotions, Expressions and Behaviors," *Journal of Retailing*, 85 (2), 222–237.

McDonald, Malcolm, Tony Millman, and Beth Rogers (1997), "Key Account Management: Theory, Practice and Challenges," *Journal of Marketing Management*, 13(8), 737–757.

McDougall, Gordon H.G. and Terrence Levesque (2000), "Customer Satisfaction With Services: Putting Perceived Value Into the Equation," *Journal of Services Marketing*, 14 (4/5), 392–410.

Meyer, Christopher and Andre Schwager (2007), "Understanding Customer Experience," *Harvard Business Review*, 85 (2), 117–126.

Meyer Goldstein, Susan, Robert Johnston, Jo A. Duffy, and Jay Rao (2002), "The Service Concept: The Missing Link in Service Design Research?," *Journal of Operations Management*, 20 (2), 121–134.

Michaels, N. (2013), *The Customer Experience: A Strategic Differentiator in Claims*. Ernst&Young.

Mittal, V., Kumar, P., and Tsiros, M. (1999), "Attribute-level performance, satisfaction, and behavioral intentions over time: a consumption-system approach," *The Journal of Marketing*, 88–101.

Mittal, Vikas, Akin Sayrak, Pandu Tadikamalla, and Eugene W. Anderson (2005), "Dual Emphasis and the Long-Term Financial Impact of Customer Satisfaction," *Marketing Science*, 24 (4), 544–555.

Moore, Gary C. and Izak Benbasat (1999), "Development of an Instrument to Measure the Perceptions of Adopting an Information Technology Innovation," *Information Systems Research*, 2 (3), 192–222.

Morgan, H., H. Purchase, S. Flatto, and D. Sanderson (2013), Creating Outstanding Customer Experiences in Shopping Centres: BCSC.

Mossberg, Lena (2007), "A Marketing Approach to the Tourist Experience," *Scandinavian Journal of Hospitality and Tourism*, 7 (1), 59–74.

Murray, Kyle B. and Steven Bellman (2011), "Productive Play Time: How Consumers Optimize Hedonic Experiences," *Journal of the Academy of Marketing Science*, 39 (3), 376–391.

Nambisan, Priya and James H. Watt (2011), "Managing Customer Experiences in Online Product Communities," *Journal of Business Research*, 64 (3), 889–895.

Neely, Andy (2008), "Exploring the financial consequences of the servitization of manufacturing," *Operations Management Research*, 1(2), 103–118.

Neslin, S. A., Grewal, D., Leghorn, R., Shankar, V., Teerling, M. L., Thomas, J. S., and Verhoef, P. C. (2006), "Challenges and opportunities in multichannel customer management," *Journal of Service Research*, 9 (2), 95–112.

Niederkrotenthaler, T., Voracek, M., Herberth, A., Till, B., Strauss, M., Etzersdorfer, E., Eisenwort, B., and Sonneck, G. (2010), "Role of Media Reports in Completed and Prevented Suicide: Werther v. Papageno Effects," *The British Journal of Psychiatry*, September, 197 (3), 234–243, doi: 10.1192/bjp.bp.109.074633.

Oracle (2012), *Eight Steps to Great Customer Experiences for Government Agencies,* Oracle.

Ortinau, David J. (2010), "Primer for New Authors: On the Fundamentals of Publishing in Marketing Journals," *Journal of Marketing Theory and Practice,* 18 (1), 91–100.

Palmer, Adrian (2010), "Customer Experience Management: A Critical Review of an Emerging Idea," *Journal of Services Marketing,* 24 (3), 196–208.

Parasuraman, A., Leonard L. Berry, and Valarie A. Zelthaml (1993), "More on Improving Service Quality Measurement," *Journal of Retailing,* 69 (Spring), 140–147.

Parasuraman, A., Valarie A. Zeithaml, and Arvind Malhotra (2005), "E-S-QUAL: A Multiple-item Scale for Assessing Electronic Service Quality," *Journal of Service Research,* 7 (3), 213–234.

Parasuraman, A., Valarie A. Zeithaml, and Leonard L. Berry (1994), "Alternative Scales for Measuring Service Quality: A Comparative Assessment Based on Psychometric and Diagnostic Criteria," *Journal of Retailing,* 70 (3), 201–230.

Parasuraman, A., Valarie A. Zeithaml, and Leonard L. Berry (1988), "SERVQUAL: A Multiple-item Scale for Measuring Consumer Perceptions," *Journal of Retailing,* 64 (1), 12–40.

Parsons, Talcott (1934), "Some Reflections on the Nature and Significance of Economics," *Quarterly Journal of Economics,* 48 (3), 511–545.

Patrício, Lia, Raymond P. Fisk, and Larry Constantine (2011), "Multilevel Service Design: From Customer Value Constellation to Service Experience Blueprinting," *Journal of Service Research,* 14 (2), 180–200.

Payne, Adrian and Pennie Frow (2005), "A Strategic Framework for Customer Relationship Management," *Journal of Marketing,* 69 (4), 167–176.

Payne, Adrian, Kay Storbacka, and Pennie Frow (2008), "Managing the Co-creation of Value," *Journal of the Academy of Marketing Science,* 36 (1), 83–96.

Pine, B. Joseph and James Gilmore (1998), "Welcome to the Experience Economy," *Harvard Business Review,* 76 (4), 97–105.

Pine, B. Joseph and James Gilmore (1999), *The Experience Economy: Work is Theatre and Every Business a Stage,* Cambridge, MA: Harvard Business School Press.

Polit, Denis F. (1996), "Factor Analysis," in D. F. Polit (ed.), *Data Analysis and Statistics for Nursing Research,* Stamford, CT: Appleton and Lange, 345–379.

Ponsignon, Fred, Klaus, Philipp, and Maull, Roger (forthcoming), "Service Experience Engineering (SEE): A Critical Examination of Service Experience Management Practices in Financial Services Organizations," *Journal of Service Management.*

Prahalad, Coimbatore K. and Hamel, G. (1990), The core competence of the corporation. *Boston (MA),* 235–256.

Prahalad, Coimbatore K. and Venkat Ramaswamy (2004), "Co-creation Experiences: The Next Practice in Value Creation," *Journal of Interactive Marketing*, 18 (3), 5–14.

Privette, Gayle (1983), "Peak Experience, Peak Performance, and Flow," *Journal of Personality and Social Psychology*, 45 (6), 1361–1368.

Puccinelli, Nancy M., Roland C. Goodstein, Dhruv Grewal, Robert Price, Priya Raghubir, and Davis Stewart (2009), "Customer Experience Management in Retailing: Understanding the Buying Process," *Journal of Retailing*, 85 (1), 15–30.

Pugh, Derek S., David J. Hickson, and Christopher R. Hinings (1969), "An Empirical Taxonomy of Structures of Work Organizations," *Administrative Science Quarterly*, 14, 115–126.

Pullman, Madeleine E. and Michael A. Gross (2004), "Ability of Experience Design Elements to Elicit Emotions and Loyalty Behaviors," *Decision Sciences*, 35 (3), 551–578.

Rawson, Alex, Ewan Duncan, and Conor Jones (2013), "The Truth about Customer Experience," *Harvard Business Review*, 91 (9), 90–98.

Ray, Michael (1973), "Marketing Communication and the Hierarchy of Effects," in Clarke (ed.), *New Models for Communication Research*, Beverly Hills, CA: SAGE, pp. 146–175.

Reichheld, Frederick (2003), "The One Number You Need to Grow," *Harvard Business Review*, 81 (12), 46–54.

Reichheld, Frederick (2006), "The Ultimate Question," *Harvard Business School Press, Boston, MA*.

Reichheld, Frederik and W. Earl Sasser (1990), "Zero Defections: Quality Comes to Services," *Harvard Business Review*, 68 (5), 105–111.

Reinartz, Werner, Manfred Krafft, and Wayne D. Hoyer (2004), "The Customer Relationship Management Process: Its Measurement and Impact on Performance," *Journal of Marketing Research*, 41 (3), 293–305.

Reynolds, Thomas J., Charles E. Gengler, and Daniel J. Howard (1995), "The Means-end Analysis of Brand Persuasion Through Advertising," *International Journal of Research in Marketing*, 12 (3), 257–266.

Romesburg, Charles H. (1984), *Cluster Analysis for Researchers*, Belmont, CA: Lifetime Learning Publications.

Roper, Stuart, and Gary Davies (2007), "The Corporate Brand: Dealing with Multiple Stakeholders," *Journal of Marketing Management*, 23 (1–2), 75–90.

Rose, Susan, Moira Clark, Phillip Samouel, and Neil Hair (2012), "Online Customer Experience in e-Retailing: An Empirical Model of Antecedents and Outcomes," *Journal of Retailing*, 88 (2), 308–322.

Rust, Roland T., Tim Ambler, Gregory S. Carpenter, V. Kumar, and Rejendra K. Srivastava (2004), "Measuring Marketing Productivity: Current Knowledge and Future Directions," *Journal of Marketing*, 68 (4), 76–89.

Ryan, Gery W. and H. Russell Bernard (2003), "Techniques to Identify Themes," *Field Methods*, 15 (1), 85–109.

Samuel, Yitzhak and Bilha F. Mannheim (1970), "A Multidimensional Approach toward a Typology of Bureaucracy," *Administrative Science Quarterly*, 15, 216–229.

Schatzki, Theodore R. (1996), *Social Practices: A Wittgensteinian Approach to Human Activity and the Social*, Cambridge: Cambridge University Press.

Schembri, Sharon (2006), "Rationalizing Service Logic, or Understanding Services as Experience?" *Marketing Theory*, 6 (3), 381–392.

Schembri, Sharon (2009), "Reframing Brand Experience: The Experiential Meaning of Harley-Davidson," *Journal of Business Research*, 62 (12), 1299–1310.

Schmitt, Bernd H. (1999), *Experiential Marketing: How to Get Customers to Sense, Feel, Think, Act and Relate to Your Company and Brands*. New York, NY: Free Press.

Schmitt, Bernd H. (1999), "Experiential Marketing," *Journal of Marketing Management*, 15 (1–3), 53–67.

Schmitt, Bernd H. (2003), *Customer Experience Management*. Hoboken, NJ: Wiley.

Schmitt, Bernd H. (2003), *Experience Management: A Revolutionary Approach to Connecting with Your Customers*, John Wiley & Sons, Hoboken, NJ.

Schouten, John W., James H. McAlexander, and Harold F. Koenig (2007), "Transcendent Service Experience and Brand Community," *Journal of the Academy of Marketing Science*, 35 (3), 357–368.

Seiders, Kathleen, Glenn B. Voss, Dhruv Grewal, and Andrea L. Godfrey (2005), "Do Satisfied Customers Buy More? Examining Moderating Influences in a Retailing Context," *Journal of Marketing*, 69 (4), 26–43.

Shankar, Venkatesh, Amy K. Smith, and Arvind Rangaswamy (2003), "Customer Satisfaction and Loyalty in Online and Offline Environments," *International Journal of Research in Marketing*, 20 (2), 153–175.

Sharma, N., and Patterson, P. G. (1999), "The impact of communication effectiveness and service quality on relationship commitment in consumer, professional services," *Journal of services marketing*, 13 (2), 151–170.

Sharma, N., and Patterson, P. G. (2000), "Switching costs, alternative attractiveness and experience as moderators of relationship commitment in professional, consumer services," *International journal of service industry management*, 11 (5), 470–490.

Silvestro, Rhian (1999), "Positioning Services Along the Volume-variety Diagonal: The Contingencies of Service Design, Control and Improvement," *International Journal of Operations and Production Management*, 19 (4), 399–421.

Silvestro, Rhian, Lin Fitzgerald, Robert Johnston, and Christopher Voss (1992), "Towards a Classification of Service Processes," *International Journal of Service Industry Management*, 3 (3), 62–75.

Söderlund, Magnus (2002), "Customer Familiarity and Its Effects on Satisfaction and Behavioral Intentions," *Psychology and Marketing*, 19 (10), 861–880.

Springer, T., D. Azzarello and J. Melton (2011). *What It Takes to Win with Customer Experience*: Bain & Company.

Spohrer, Jim, Paul P. Maglio, John Bailey, and Danial Gruhl (2007), "Steps Toward a Science of Service Systems," *Computer*, 40 (January), 71–77.

Statistical Innovation (2011), *7.1 Tutorial #1: Using Latent GOLD 4.0 to Estimate LC Cluster Models*, available at: http://statisticalinnovations.com/products/LGtutorial1.pdf.

Statistical Innovation (2011), *Latent GOLD 4.5: About Latent Class Modelling*, available at: http://statisticalinnovations.com/products/aboutlc.html.

Statistical Innovations (2011), *Tutorial #6A: Comparing Segments obtained from LC Cluster and DFactor Models in a Consumer Preference Study DemoData = "crackers0. sav,"* Available at: http://statisticalinnovations.com/products/LGtutorial6A.pdf based on Popper, Richard, Jeff Kroll, and Jay Magidson (2004), "Applications of Latent Class Models to Food Product Development: A Case Study," *Sawtooth Software Proceedings*, 2004, Available at: http://www.statisticalinnovations. com/technicalsupport/popper.pdf.

Strauss, Anselm (1987), *Qualitative Analysis for Social Scientists*, Cambridge, UK: Cambridge University Press.

Strauss, Anselm C. and Luliet M. Corbin (1990), *Basics of Qualitative Research: Grounded Theory Procedures and Techniques*, Newbury Park, CA: SAGE.

Sweeney, Jillian C., Geoffrey N. Soutar (2001), "Customer Perceived Value: The Development of a Multiple Item Scale," *Journal of Retailing*, 77 (2), 203–220.

Sweeney, Jillian C., Geoffrey N. Soutar, and Lester W. Johnson (1999), "The Role of Perceived Risk in the Quality-value Relationship: A Study in a Retail Environment," *Journal of Retailing*, 75 (1), 77–105.

Tabachnick, Barbara G. and Linda S. Fidell (1996), *Using Multivariate Statistics*, Third edition, New York, NY: Harper Collins.

Tammo, H. A. Bijmolt, Leo J. Paas, and Jeroen K. Vermunt (2003), "Country and consumer segmentation: multi-level latent class analysis of financial product ownership," *Discussion Paper*, Tillburg University, Accessed: http://statisticalinnovations. com/products/multilevel_country.pdf.

Tapio, Petri (2003). "Disaggregative Policy Delphi: Using Cluster Analysis as a Tool for Systematic Scenario Formation," *Technological Forecasting and Social Change*, 70 (1), 83–101.

Thacker, James W., Mitchell W. Fields, and Lois E. Tetrick (1989), "The Factor Structure of Union Commitment: An Application of Confirmatory Factor Analysis," *Journal of Applied Psychology*, 74 (2), 228–232.

TU World Telecommunication/ICT Indicators database (2014).

Tynan, Caroline, Sally McKechnie, and Celine Chhuon (2010), "Co-creating Value for Luxury Brands," *Journal of Business Research*, 63 (11), 1156–1163.

Van Doorn, J., and Verhoef, P. C. (2008), "Critical incidents and the impact of satisfaction on customer share," *Journal of Marketing*, 72 (4), 123–142.

Vargo, Stephen L. and Robert F. Lusch (2004), "Evolving to a New Dominant Logic for Marketing," *Journal of Marketing*, 68 (1), 1–17.

Vargo, Stephen L. and Robert F. Lusch (2008), "From Goods to Service(s): Divergences and Convergences of Logics," *Industrial Marketing Management*, 37 (3), 254–259.

Verhoef, Peter C. (2003), "Understanding the Effect of Customer Relationship Management Efforts on Customer Retention and Customer Share Development," *Journal of Marketing*, 67 (4), 30–45.

Verhoef, Peter C., Katherine N. Lemon, A. Parasuraman, Anne Roggeveen, Michael Tsiros, and Leonard A. Schlesinger (2009), "Customer Experience: Determinants, Dynamics and Management Strategies," *Journal of Retailing*, 85 (1), 31–41.

Voss, Christopher, Aleda V. Roth, and Richard B. Chase (2008), "Experience, Service Operations Strategy, and Services as Destinations: Foundations and Exploratory Investigation," *Production and Operations Management*, 17 (3), 247–66.

Voss, Christopher and Leonieke Zomerdijk (2007), "Innovation in Experiential Services – An Empirical View," in DTI (ed.), *Innovation in Services*, London, UK: DTI, pp. 97–134.

Walsh, Gianfranco and Sharon E. Beatty (2007), "Customer-based Corporate Reputation of the Service Firm: Scale Development and Validation," *Journal of the Academy of Marketing Science*, 35 (1), 127–143.

Webster Jr., Frederick E. and Yoram Wind (1972), "A General Model for Understanding Organizational Buying Behavior," *Journal of Marketing*, 36 (2), 12–19.

Westbrook, Robert A. (1987), "Product/Consumption-Based Affective Responses and Postpurchase Processes," *Journal of Marketing Research*, 24 (3), 258–270.

Womack, James and Daniel T. Jones (2005), *Lean Solutions*, New York: Free Press.

Woodruff, Robert B. (1997), "Customer value: The Next Source for Competitive Advantage," *Journal of the Academy of Marketing Science*, 25 (2), 139–153.

Woodruff, Robert B. and Daniel J. Flint (2006), "Marketing's Service Dominant Logic and Customer Value," in S. L. Vargo and R. F. Lusch (eds), *Toward a Service-Dominant Logic of Marketing: Dialog, Debate, and Directions*, New York, NY: M.E. Sharpe, pp. 183–195.

World Bank (2009), *World Development Report 2009 – Reshaping Economic Geography,* Washington, DC: The World Bank.

Yi, Youjae and Suana La (2004), "What Influences the Relationship Between Customer Satisfaction and Repurchase Intention? Investigating the Effects of Adjusted Expectations and Customer Loyalty," *Psychology and Marketing*, 21 (5), 351–373.

Zeithaml, Valarie A. (1988), "Consumer Perceptions of Price, Quality, and Value: A Means-end Model and Synthesis of Evidence," *Journal of Marketing*, 52 (3), 2–22.

Zeithaml, Valarie A., Leonard L. Berry, and A. Parasuraman (1996), "The Behavioral Consequences of Service Quality," *Journal of Marketing*, 60 (2), 31–46.

Zeithaml, Valarie A. (2000), "Service quality, profitability, and the economic worth of customers: what we know and what we need to learn," *Journal of the Academy of Marketing Science*, 28 (1), 67–85.

Zeithaml, Valarie A., Ruth N. Bolton, John Deighton, Timothy L. Keiningham, Katherine N. Lemon, and J. Andrew Petersen (2006), "Forward Looking Focus: Can Firms Have Adaptive Foresight?" *Journal of Service Research*, 9 (2), 168–183.

Index

Printed and bound by CPI Group (UK) Ltd, Croydon, CR0 4YY